SURVIVAL AND LOVE

Double Escape from the Nazis

Lizzy and George Dyszkiewicz

Author

Ted Bailey

Grosvenor House
Publishing Limited

This book is published by
Grosvenor House Publishing Ltd
Link House
140 The Broadway, Tolworth, Surrey, KT6 7HT.
www.grosvenorhousepublishing.co.uk

A CIP record for this book
is available from the British Library

ISBN 978-1-78623-632-6

CONTENTS

ACKNOWLEDGEMENTS

My thanks to Nicky Cirillo for bringing these first-hand experiences to my attention. Forming them into a coherent story was imperative for both the personal and the historical record.

I also want to thank her mother, Lizzy Dyszkiewicz, for agreeing to meet me and supplying photos from her personal archive which have helped to augment the written word.

ILLUSTRATIONS

PREFACE

Life produces many coincidences. One of the most bizarre occurred on a visit to my osteopath. We both share a keen interest in family history and we tend to talk about this quite a lot during treatment. Previously, I had published a book about my grandfather's military career in the Great War and she asked if I had any other similar ventures in the offing. Coincidentally, I was indeed searching around for some inspiration to write something else.

At this point she told me that a good friend of hers had a very interesting story to tell about her mother's experiences in World War Two. Was I interested? Indeed, my curiosity was aroused. She then handed me a single sheet of paper. On both sides, in tightly arranged type, was a succinct but very moving account of teenage Lizzy Schwarz's miraculously lucky survival from several Nazi concentration camps, sadly unlike the rest of her family.

As I read it, I was immediately convinced that this was a story that just had to be shared widely for the public record. As the person chosen to be the narrator of her mother Lizzy's summary of Holocaust survival, I had to weave this into a proper story that captured the deeply profound nature of her experience in some order and set it in its historical context, namely the most horrendous conditions in war-torn Europe.

There was a happy ending to this horror: eventual survival, love and happiness in London. Whilst starting to arrange the story of Lizzy into a coherent sequence, it emerged that she coincidentally met a Polish Army Cadet after the war, one Jerzy Dyszkiewicz, the man who eventually became her husband. Surprisingly, he too had a similar story of lucky war experiences which were in the best tradition of Prisoner of War (POW) escapes. Jerzy, now George, had a taped account record of this and I felt it was imperative that it be included as a story of parallel luck.

As the person chosen to write up these authentic personal experiences and put them into historical context for the reader, it has been a privilege to do so. There are a host of holocaust stories and daredevil POW escape stories and so, perhaps with the inevitable passage of time, they may begin to fade into a shadowy world of the past and seem to be less relevant to our contemporary world. Nothing could or indeed *should* be further from the truth. Despite the passage of time they must always remain in the front of our consciousness. This particularly applies to all stories about the horrendous suffering visited by that odious Nazi state on the Jews and many other victims of their vile racist policies. All these accounts deserve to be as widely known as possible for they contribute authentic personal insights as vital entries to the overall historical record of that period.

As the author, I have listened carefully to what Lizzy and George have expressed about their experiences and in the writing of this narrative have tried to recapture their feelings and the events as authentically as possible. Both told of their experiences in their own way. Lizzy was surprisingly detached about what was obviously an horrendous teenage period and in George's case, he was often very specific and so I have quoted him directly. Where I directly quote his words, they are in *italics*.

I was lucky enough to meet Lizzy while conducting my research into her first-hand sources and she verified the various photographs which appear here and clarified some facts which helped me get a better overall view. It is nigh impossible to imagine being in someone else's shoes because everybody's experiences are unique to them especially in a totally different era, as in this case. However, listening to both Lizzy and George tell of their extraordinary experiences in such a matter-of-fact manner, it feels that they could have occurred only yesterday. Despite that, the impact remains powerful.

The separate stories of Lizzy and George, which constitute the core of this book, occurred in places and times very different from our own, a period of massive international upheaval in Europe and warfare. The recounting of their first-hand experiences are important historical statements because they bear witness to hope and unaccountable luck against great odds. Although these happened in different geographical circumstances, I have intermingled them in a combined table, to show their common feature: lucky survival.

Lizzy and George were remembering things from over fifty years ago by delving into their long-term memory, so inevitably, there are some gaps in their memories concerning various incidents and dates during their long tense journeys. I have conducted comprehensive background research to augment their primary inputs but there are clearly still some lapses of memory on their part. These must unfortunately remain in the sphere of what I have elsewhere called 'unavailable history'. However, these gaps in memory in no way detract from the overall narrative of their lucky escapes which even today remain powerful.

Finally, I take responsibility for my interpretation of all the facts therein.

....

INTRODUCTION

This is a remarkable story from World War Two which starts out in two separate places but is linked by a common thread of time involving two people who are totally different in nationality, culture, religion and ethnic group but who coincidentally share life-changing experiences brought about by mass upheaval, invasion and large scale war.

In 1939, Lizzy Schwarz was a teenage Czechoslovakian Jew and Jerzy Dyszkiewicz a teenage Polish Officer Cadet. What follows is a true account by our two protagonists which describes their fateful and unrelated journeys across war-torn Europe, as told to others many years later.

However, what is uplifting throughout this whole narrative is that they were both repeatedly blessed with the luckiest escapes of their lives. They were buffeted by forces beyond their control being swept along into dangerous life-threatening journeys, with one travelling eastwards and the other westwards.

In Lizzy's case, these outside influences were completely proscriptive as she was consistently dragged along completely at the mercy of Nazi racial policy and camp life. Lizzy Schwarz lived in Moravia, one of the constituent regions of the then Czechoslovakia, when the German Army illegitimately invaded and occupied her country in March 1939. Czechoslovakia was one of the new states that had been established from the disintegration and collapse of the Habsburg Dynasty of Austria-Hungary in the chaos that followed the end of the First World War in 1918. It had now become part of the Nazi plan for the creation of a new Pan-Germanic Eastern Europe. From that moment of the occupation, Lizzy's idyllic rural life in her small hilly town of Boskovice was completely and irrevocably changed with disastrous consequences for her and her family.

The Jews of Boskovice were now subject to the new German Protectorate of Bohemia and Moravia as the country was sub-divided to suit Hitler's plans in the East. The odious racial policies of the ruling Nazi Party, initially witnessed in Germany when Adolf Hitler came to power as the Leader in 1933, were now visited upon Czechoslovakia. These policies were based on the notion of the Aryan race, predominantly Western Europeans and epitomised by the German Nazis who saw themselves as the 'master race'. This meant that all other ethnic groups were inferior and among those that the Nazis regarded as the *untermensch* (under-people) the Jews were specifically targeted. It was not long before things escalated in the mass rounding up and transportation of them to the concentration camps.

Among the resident Jews of Boskovice, Lizzy's family was shipped off to Terezin, north of Prague, where the transit and ghetto camp of Theresienstadt was established.

Unlike the remainder of her family who all eventually perished in the concentration camps, Lizzy's story is one of most amazingly lucky survivals. After being interned in several of the most notorious killing camps throughout those dreadful years her survival was, in her own words, by the sheer luck of the draw.

Jerzy's case is different, initially he was a newly qualified member of the Polish Army Officer Cadets having just completed his year's compulsory military training. In September 1939, Nazi Germany invaded Poland on a trumped-up excuse and much to the surprise of the whole world, the Soviet Army entered the country from the East shortly afterwards. This was the result of a secret protocol signed only weeks before as part of the shocking Nazi-Soviet Non-Aggression Pact to partition Poland.

As Jerzy and his comrades marched West to meet the German enemy they were captured by the Soviets advancing from the East and transported into the Ukraine. Eventually, after a time, they were handed over to the Germans in exchange for other prisoners to be returned. From then on, Jerzy was a Prisoner of War (POW) in a series of officer camps in Germany, being moved around as part of a workforce in contradiction of the relevant Agreement as part of the Geneva Convention, including a stint at what was a 'punishment camp' in The Netherlands to instil discipline. When in Aachen, close to the border with Belgium, Jerzy and his comrades seized an opportunity and escaped, setting out on a roller coaster journey to the eventual safety of neutral Spain, thence to England.

The different experiences of these two participants in this story against the larger background history of that world war, namely the horror of the Holocaust and the derring-do of the POW escapades, are only a couple in a veritable sea of such stories but this does not detract from their importance in any way. All such accounts deserve to be as widely known as possible and fully appreciated for what they are. All these stories act as a warning for the future as the events in the breakup of Yugoslavia and even more recent European ideological and political nationalist and fascist trends clearly attest.

....

EUROPE AT WAR AGAIN

On 1 September 1939, Germany invaded Poland on a trumped-up excuse and thereby plunged Europe and eventually the world into a six-year war, the major consequences many of which are still being felt even today. On 3 September, Great Britain and France declared war on Germany, the announcement being made on BBC radio at 11.15am, those countries having failed to halt or effect the withdrawal of German troops. This was only just twenty years since the Treaty of Versailles was signed ending the previous First World War. That ghastly war, also often referred to as the Great War, was subsequently dubbed "The war to end all wars", first attributed years before to British author HG Wells. Yet here was Europe at war against Germany yet again leading to another worldwide conflagration.

For Lizzy Schwarz and her family, the declaration of war was yet one more step on the road to impending disaster after the German occupation, annexation and division of Czechoslovakia in March 1939. Over the following months the Jewish teenager who had been enjoying her life in her birth town now lived under the control of the newly organised Nazi Protectorate of Bohemia-Moravia. Her family were attempting to come to terms with this increasingly alien rule which often involved the dangerous presence of the Gestapo, the German Secret State Police. Being Jewish and seeing the treatment that Jews had already received at home in Nazi Germany and Austria, already annexed to form a Greater Germany, there was a great deal of foreboding in the Schwarz family. It could only be a matter of time before they too were on the receiving end of the same. Indeed, it was not long before life restricting rules were imposed upon the Jews of Boskovice and eventually they were rounded up and transported to a concentration camp.

For recently qualified Officer Cadet, Jerzy Dyszkiewicz and his comrades marching eastwards to meet the German invasion, there was a big surprise. On 28 September, as they proceeded along the road, they were confronted and surrounded by Soviet forces. From that time on their war, which had started with the strafing of their barracks by Luftwaffe Stukas, was over for them before they even got started.

After years of tension, devious manipulation, outright aggression and expansion during the twenties and thirties by Fascist Italy and Nazi Germany, this sudden attack on Poland was the inevitable outcome of these dangerous policies which many in the know had half expected but was still a shock to others when war started in real terms. In Poland, the expectation was that Britain and France would honour their pre-war alliance to defend Poland's independence and attack Germany in the West. Unfortunately, despite the specific promise to the Poles, particularly by France, to their utter dismay this did not happen in any realistic terms although the French did briefly threaten the Siegfried Line, the German defences, but were pushed back.

This was the second betrayal by the Western powers in allowing annexation of a sovereign territory following that of the year before when the Sudetenland part of Czechoslovakia was handed over to Germany at the Munich Agreement without any meaningful resistance, or the presence of the Czechoslovak government.

After this initial flurry of military activity, things on land in the West settled down to what was referred to as the Phoney War, a period of eight months when, apart from the odd skirmish mainly at sea, there was an uneasy stalemate between the combatants. In Britain this enabled a much-needed period when the civil authorities quickly prepared for what was the belief that air raids would follow and the rapid build-up of the previously depleted army and the Royal Air Force.

In Poland however, the success of the German invasion was far from 'phoney' but in fact exceedingly speedy and destructive as the Polish Army was swept aside in a Blitzkrieg and the country overrun within weeks. This success by the German Army was accompanied by an occupation from the East by the Soviet Union, only weeks after a shocking non-aggression pact had been signed by these two countries of opposing ideologies. By October, the country had been divided between Germany in the West and the Soviet Union in the East.

The outbreak of another war in just over twenty years immediately altered the previous precarious post World

War One status quo in Central Europe, always a key objective of Nazi Germany. Both Czechoslovakia and Poland were carved up, the former being divided in the occupation earlier that year and the latter being partitioned within a month of the start of the war.

....

LIZZY: A CAREFREE CHILDHOOD

The story of Lizzy Schwarz starts on 11 May 1927 when she was born to Moric and Hilda Schwarz, two shop owners in Boskovice in Czechoslovakia. She spent an idyllic time in this town which was set in the highlands of Moravia and where she was a happy child in her small locality set next to hilly surroundings in the countryside. She says she really enjoyed her time at primary school, had many good friends and often went to their houses for tea and similar activities that the children took part in.

Lizzy's sister was called Kitty and she was seven years older than her, being born on 11 January 1920. They got on well although obviously they did not go out and about together as Lizzy was too young for Kitty and her friends, so they obviously had different interests given their different ages. The family lived in a big house above a delicatessen shop in the main square of the town which was always crowded with customers from all backgrounds.

It was a largely rural existence in this small town and presented many opportunities for outdoor play for a child in the surrounding area. The photograph below, which could pass for a Christmas card, clearly captures

Lizzy on a sleigh in the hills around Boskovice

this winter land scene showing a very young Lizzy on a sledge in the snow-covered hills.

However, this simple happy life was not to last as when Lizzy was a teenager the army of the Nazis invaded and occupied her country in 1939. From then on, Lizzy and her family's life changed beyond imagination for one single reason: they were Jews.

Boskovice, initially called Boskovitz in German when it was part of Moravia in the Austrian side of the Austro-Hungarian Empire, is a town located just over one hundred miles south east of the capital Prague and about 21 miles north of Brno, the old capital city of Moravia. Boskovice is an historic town and dates back to early medieval times as evinced by the ruins of the thirteenth century castle and the impressive chateau, both sights attracting modern visitors.

At that time, Brno, the second largest city after the new Czechoslovakian capital Prague, had the biggest German population at 63%. Coincidentally the Jewish population of Boskovice was largely made up of the descendants of those who had been expelled from Brno in 1451. There had been a long history of anti-Semitism in many European countries including the territories of the Habsburg Empire. Czechoslovakia was one new state created from that empire by the Treaty of Versailles in 1919.

By the time of the 1920s though, many Jews in the west of the country were quite well-integrated, something confirmed by Lizzy. In 1921, Boskovice had one of the largest Jewish populations in the whole country with over 37,900 residents. Unsurprisingly, it also had one of the biggest Jewish cemeteries, dating back to the seventeenth century.

It also had a traditional self-contained Jewish Quarter, referred to as a 'ghetto', which was entered by the Jewish Gate. This pre-war ghetto had no restrictions as the residents could come and go as they pleased, unlike the cramped ghettos later established by the Nazis in World War Two, as epitomised in Warsaw.

Lizzy's family lived in Moravia (Map below), one of the three provinces of the country, the other two being: Bohemia and Slovakia.

As Lizzy became older, things were beginning to change in her social life. Whereas previously her friends greeted her unconditionally now they continued to do so in the street but did not come to the house anymore. Lizzy felt that the atmosphere had changed. Also, her parents were beginning to worry a lot as Hitler and his Nazis were looming more threateningly in the surrounding areas. He was getting nearer and nearer to their previously secure lives.

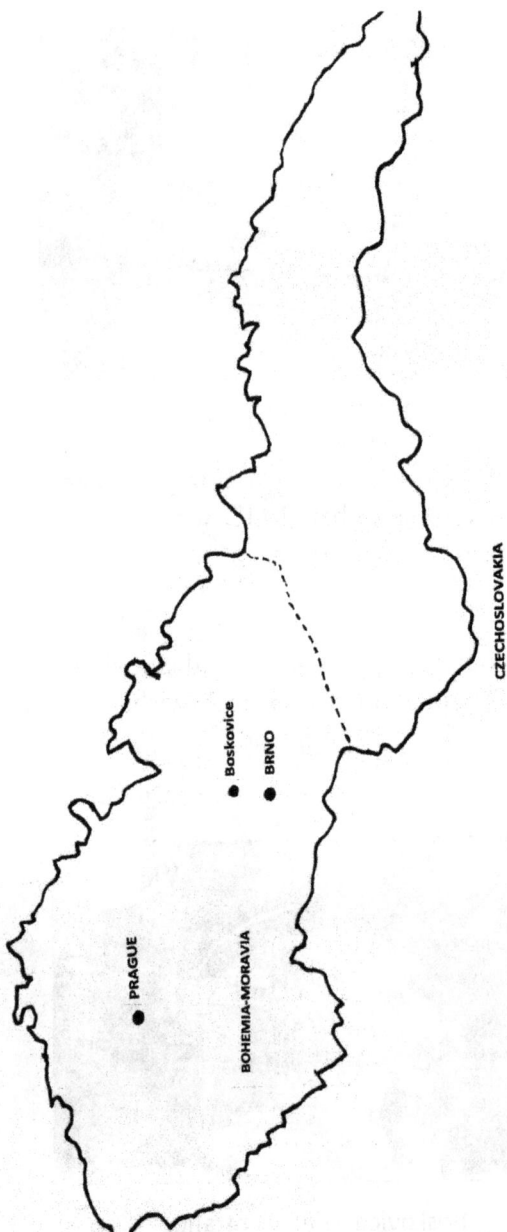

Map of Bohemia and Moravia

Pre-war Boskovice

The above postcard was sent to Lizzy by one of her teacher's on 12 December 1947 with the following message:

'Dear Lizzy
I hope that you are in good health and enjoying the new experience. Thank you for your good wishes and I hope that you will be happy in England'.

Boskovice Ghetto Entrance

A ghetto street

EUROPE BETWEEN THE WARS

The background to the increasing concerns of the Schwarz family over their national security was widely shared in the other countries of Central and Eastern Europe. It originated in the period of autocratic upheaval in Europe with the rise of rabid nationalism rising from the ashes of the Great War in November 1918. The victory of the major Allies of Britain, France and the United States led to the complete collapse of the Central Powers comprising the empires of Germany, Austria-Hungary and Ottoman Turkey. Russia's violent communist revolution in October 1917 further exacerbated the chaos.

It is the break-up of Austria-Hungary and the fall of the Habsburg dynasty which is of direct concern here. To put this in context it is necessary to briefly outline the nature of the Habsburg monarchy which dominated central Europe from the sixteenth century. One branch of the Habsburgs ruled Spain and Portugal and The Netherlands (including present day Belgium), until it ceased to exist in 1700. In the eighteenth century, through intermarriage, the other Austrian branch ruled over a vast swathe of Central Europe, initially as the Austrian Empire, then the Dual Monarchy of Austria-Hungary after 1867. Up to the end of the First World War, this entity was a vast collection of disparate territories populated by many very different ethnic and religious groups, with competing and conflicting interests and demands. As a result of losing the war the Habsburg conglomeration disintegrated and many new nations were independently created.

The years immediately after that war were characterised by continued instability as these newly formed independent states, such as Czechoslovakia and reformed Poland, struggled to address considerable national, ethnic, linguistic, economic, and racial challenges. Czechoslovakia particularly had a substantial and complex mix of very different and competing German, Polish and Lithuanian ethnic minorities who did not readily accept their position in the newly formed country, resulting from the post-war boundary decisions.

As we see in Lizzy's story, this especially applied to the Sudetenland Germans who inhabited the area in the northern, western and eastern boundaries of the country. The post-war boundary placement of this group would play a big part in a future crisis deliberately engineered by the expansionist policies of the Nazis in Germany. In addition to that, significantly, there were many thousands of Jews in the country who had previously settled there having fled the pogroms in the East in earlier centuries.

Poland, which had been recreated by the Treaty of Versailles, after its separation from the Russian empire which had collapsed in the revolution of 1917, also had pressing ethnic minority problems. Over one third of the population comprised Ukrainians, Byelorussians (now Belarussians), Jews and Germans and most of these were historically hostile to the existence of the Polish state.

It was during the 1920s that Europe saw the rise of a new strident ethnic nationalism: Fascism in Italy and Nazism in Germany. In that same decade both Jerzy and Lizzy were born into Poland and Czechoslovakia respectively and Nazism would come to shape their teenage years and propel their different journeys during World War Two.

Nazism grew from the defeat of Imperial Germany producing a profound disaffection among the army. One of the soldiers in that war was Adolf Hitler, who so despised the Habsburgs that he did not want to serve in their army, although he was born in Austria. At the outbreak of war, benefitting from an administrative error, he enlisted in the German Army instead and ended the war as a Corporal. He had lived in Vienna prior to the war as a budding but unsuccessful artist. Vienna, then the capital of the Austro-Hungarian Empire, was a cosmopolitan multi-ethnic city with a large Jewish population. It was during this period that he developed the anti-Semitic ideology that would later become influential and be a crucial factor enabling him to finally take power in Germany in 1933.

As the war ended in November 1918, the German Kaiser William II fled to neutral Holland and a new republic was declared at Weimar which gave its name to it. However, many of the army who opposed the republic, including Hitler, subscribed to what became known as the 'stab in the back' myth. This right-wing view held that Germany had not actually been defeated in the battlefield (after a gargantuan effort by the Allies, it had) but had been subverted at home by civilians, Jews and Marxists, regarded as the corrupt pillars of the new republic, dubbed "the November criminals". The Treaty of Versailles imposed heavy reparations on Germany and severely limited its military capacity. The terms of the treaty were regarded as humiliating and only added to the myth that this great power had been betrayed from the home front.

Resulting from his youthful experiences in pre-war Vienna and compounded by his view of the defeat of Germany, Hitler joined the newly formed National Socialist German Workers Party in 1920, known later as the Nazis and very quickly became its leader shifting it a long way from the socialism in its name. The party members were predominantly veterans of the war who were involved in paramilitary activity, especially against the *Bolsheviks* (communists). The Bolsheviks were the party who eventually seized power in the chaos of the Russian Revolution of October 1917. Their ideas spread widely after the war as many people of the pre-war empires sought alternative radical democratic socialist solutions to government. This was the case in Germany where Russian style workers' councils, or Soviets in Russian, were being set up to form local governments in major cities, leading to conflict with right-wing opposition in the streets.

At the forefront of this unofficial street war were the Nazis who were highly organised and travelled round in open top trucks terrorising and literally beating up any opposition, but particularly the Bolsheviks. It was but a small step for the Nazis to conflate the Jews with the dreaded enemy of Bolshevism. Nazi ideology contended that the October 1917 Bolshevik Revolution in Russia was financed and dominated by Jews and that they were involved in the decline and defeat of Germany at the end of the Great War. Therefore, Jews were clearly identified as the main 'enemies of the state' as they were now seen to be constantly engaged in a Jewish-Bolshevik plot using international finance to dominate the pure Aryan race characterised by most Germans. This Nazi paranoia ramped up by Hitler's increasingly poisonous antisemitic rhetoric in his public speeches had devastating consequences in real terms when the Nazis came to power in 1933.

From the outset, the Nazis immediately set about eradicating those they designated as 'political enemies' and subversives. These were the communists, Social Democrats, Trade Unionists and repeat criminals interned without trial initially in specialised concentration camps for 're-education', the first being at Dachau outside Munich. During this so-called re-education the internees were subjected to the harshest of treatment: regular severe beatings, heavy labour, starvation diet, torture and often summary execution.

The Jews were next. Immediately they were subjected to increasing physical and legal restrictions in their public lives eventually resulting in segregation. Things got much worse later in the thirties as the Nazi racial policy was enshrined in the Nuremburg Laws which completely prohibited Jews from marrying or having extramarital intercourse with Germans and forbade the employment of Jewish women under 45 in German households. Worse was to come as the Nazis extended their persecution to other 'out groups', Gypsies, Slavs, the disabled, homosexuals, prostitutes, beggars, in fact *any* group that opposed and threatened their beliefs in the racial superiority of the native Germans.

Also, since the 1920s behind the scenes, Hitler had been preparing his policy for expansion (*Lebensraum* or living space) into Eastern Europe, especially Poland and Russia. This early twentieth century idea was offered as a way of supplementing much-needed raw materials by colonising agricultural land. It was realised as a practical solution in 1914-18 when the Germans fought in Russia and gained much territory. After the Russian Revolution it became a specific goal that could only be implemented by conquest. As mentioned previously, in Hitler's mind communists and Jews were interchangeable and had to be destroyed as the biggest threat to Nazi Germany. During World War Two the Nazi racial policies were transported into the countries invaded and occupied. The Jews and Slavs, especially Poles living in those areas, were declared as inferior peoples and to be eliminated on a massive scale.

....

NAZI EXPANSION

The pre-invasion antisemitic racial policy produced a legitimate fear building up on the part of the Jews in Czechoslovakia who had watched how their fellows were being treated from the very moment Adolf Hitler became Chancellor of Germany in 1933. Thereafter, Hitler's infamous Nazi Storm Troopers (Sturmabteilung or SA) who had played a big part in his rise to power began to rampage throughout the land attacking anyone who was not part of the Aryan race, particularly Jews. As observed, anti-Jewish sanctions and laws were brought in which made the life of the German Jewish population increasingly unbearable. Another significant development occurred in 1934 when the Storm Troopers were ruthlessly eradicated and replaced by the even more infamous Schutzstaffel (SS), a paramilitary organisation that started out as originally Hitler's bodyguard. Eventually, some of their units would be responsible for the extermination of the Jews and other perceived undesirables.

Not only at home, there were signs of future omens abroad as the Nazis backtracked on all the post-war treaties. In March 1936, the German army marched into the demilitarised zone of the Rhineland, which had been designed to provide a neutral barrier between

France and Germany after World War One. The western powers made much noise in protest but did nothing. Emboldened by this lack of action, in March 1938, after long term instigation by the local Nazis they marched unopposed into Austria and incorporated it into what Austrian-born Adolf Hitler termed 'Greater Germany'.

As a result, many thousands of Jews fled Austria into Czechoslovakia and settled in Brno. However, despite the raised tension in Europe and the distaste that many had about the Nazis and their reprehensible behaviour towards the Jews and other 'out groups', there did not seem to be a real reason to feel that any of this would directly affect Lizzy's family in an independent Czechoslovakia. At this point they had no idea how quickly this supposed security would unravel and bring the fear closer to home.

Perhaps the most ominous early warning sign as to how the Nazis would treat the Jews in Europe was *Kristallnacht* or 'Night of Broken Glass' in November 1938, with the glass shards that gave it its name littering the streets, an explicit sign of future intention and policy. The cynical pretext for this anti-Jewish 'pogrom' was the fatal shooting in Paris of a German diplomat by a Polish-Jewish German born Jew whose parents had been deported. In Germany, the trumped-up reaction of the sledgehammer wielding Nazis resulted in a dreadful price for the Jews. They ransacked Jewish shops, synagogues, hospitals and schools in a night of extreme violence. The price was high: an estimated death toll of hundreds with over 1,000 synagogues burned down and 7,000 businesses damaged or destroyed. At this point many more Jewish families decided it was time to leave Hitler's so-called Greater Germany and many made their arrangements accordingly.

The international situation now deteriorated rapidly and began to impinge upon Czechoslovakia. In the early part of 1938 Hitler had started to make demands on behalf of the predominantly ethnic Germans in Sudetenland largely located on the border of Bohemia and Moravia. This was yet again part of a devious and deliberate provocation in conjunction with the Nazi-supporting Sudeten German Party to annex this area on the pretext they were merely returning their countrymen to their rightful place in the 'Fatherland'.

There were three million ethnic Germans living in Sudetenland in north western Czechoslovakia and Hitler wanted to annex this territory ostensibly to bring these Germans into his Greater Germany and place his army there. He said in public that this was to be his 'last territorial demand'. Really this was yet another callous and devious plan to weaken the country as all the major fortifications and industries were located within that region and with his army in control there, the rest of Czechoslovakia would be virtually defenceless. This annexation of Sudetenland was only the ploy for later invasion.

Hitler had cleverly picked his time. After the occupation of the Demilitarised Rhineland had been roundly condemned by Britain and France but no action taken, he was pretty sure he could get away with this next quest. He was again 'chancing his arm', as we would say today.

Within the European Allies, after the horrors of the Great War, there was a widespread desire by the majority of their populations to avoid repeating the experience which had left most families with dreadful losses.

France, which had previously signed an Alliance with Czechoslovakia to offer military support was resigned to go to the edge and fight but was hoping not to have to. The USSR also had a pledge to do the same with France but was in an internal crisis produced by Stalinist purges of the army. In the view of the British Government it was best to adopt a policy of *appeasement* towards the German demands by negotiation to avoid the threat of conflict for which the country was completely unprepared.

To try to resolve this crisis, the British Prime Minister Neville Chamberlain took the initiative and called for a conference involving the participants: Chamberlain, Hitler, Italian leader Benito Mussolini and Édouard Daladier, the French Premier in Munich. Without British resolve to challenge Hitler head on, France went along with the conference and abandoned the Czechs.

Ironically, the crisis was averted by Mussolini who introduced an intermediary paper which enabled agreement on terms by all parties, signed in September 1938 whereby Germany was able to annexe this territory without resistance. This was successfully accomplished by an ultimatum to the Czechs who were given the choice of resisting or allowing annexation even though they were absent from the conference which determined their fate! The casual handing over of a sovereign territory was nothing short of a betrayal by Britain and France. Chamberlain returned to Britain waving a piece of paper at Croydon Airport saying this represented "peace in our time" receiving great cheers from the gathered crowd. With universal relief he clearly thought this agreement was between men of their word. This delusion was costly to both Czechoslovakia and Europe and has since been seen by most historical commentators as the last chance to stop Hitler's inexorable march onto ultimate expansion and war.

Yet more Jewish families now fled from newly German occupied Sudetenland into adjacent Czechoslovakia.

....

OCCUPATION AND TRANSPORTATION

The idyllic rural life that the growing Lizzy had was rudely interrupted by the sudden German occupation of Czechoslovakia in March 1939. Moravia became part of a Nazi Protectorate of Bohemia-Moravia. Long overdue, Britain and France finally realised that Hitler and his Nazis were devious immoral liars with absolutely no intention of observing international law. The realisation of the ease with which the Germans had overrun the whole country came too late as the time to address had been in the annexation of Sudetenland.

During this time of upheaval, an Englishman, Nicholas Winterton (among others) started to arrange for the transportation of Jewish children on trains hired specially for the purpose. This *Kindertransport* saved many Jewish children from Germany, Austria and the occupied Czechoslovakia between Kristallnacht in November 1938 and the outbreak of war in September 1939. Sadly, a group of 250 children who were due to leave Prague on 1 September were unable to do so just as the borders were closed.

The total number of children saved from the Nazis was about 10,000, 7,500 being Jewish. Among those children saved were many who subsequently became notable in adult life, of four of whom were Nobel Prize winners and many others who became significant scientists, artists and doctors.

Life for Lizzy was now to be very different from her previous rural enjoyments. She recounts that she was thirteen in 1940 when she was suddenly surprised to be banned from attending the local school that she enjoyed so much. To compensate, her parents sent her off to a Jewish Gymnasium in Brno and she was there from August 1941 to March 1942. During her time there she studied English with all the other usual subjects and activities. She managed to travel home at weekends on the train but also often came home during the week without a permit which was very dangerous if she had been caught. She was very lucky. She then joined the Maccabi Club in Boskovice and played table tennis, other sports, and went for walks. It was a good time there for her and she also went regularly to the cinema. Then the Germans closed the club in 1942 and that was that.

Also, in December 1940, her father was called into the Gestapo (State Security Police) Headquarters in Brno with no reason given. Two men in long leather overcoats turned up and took him away. The family were all very worried because this usually meant trouble and they worried they may not ever see him again. But then he returned but he never ever said anything about what had gone on. Lizzy subsequently thought it was to preserve them from knowing what was going on. During this time her mother was beginning to suffer from heart problems probably from the stress and anxiety.

Lizzy's father Moric, pre-1940

On 1 September 1941 the Germans commandeered the family's shop and the house and Lizzy's family were thrown out of there. They had to move to the back streets of the town housed in the Jewish ghetto and live there in a small flat as Jews were now not allowed to live in prominent places.

In the same month all Jews were now required to wear a yellow star in public. This was to stigmatise them and humiliate them in the eyes of everyone else. Sometimes, this caused problems if they changed clothes and forgot to sew the star on to the new clothing and went out without it. They would be in big trouble. Lizzy said that in the end it was better to have some different ones on all the clothes to stay on the safe side.

Shortly after this, all the Jews in the outlying areas were made to move into the centre of Boskovice ready for deportation. They were initially interned in the hall of a big hotel in Brno sleeping on the floor next to each other among all the internees. They lived in constant fear of the regular visits by young Nazi soldiers who required everyone to jump up to attention whenever they appeared.

Lizzy's mother Hilda had a heart condition which had emerged two years earlier and it was now getting much worse. This precluded her getting up quickly so as she naturally struggled to get up so she was shouted at and kicked by a young SS man. This was bad enough but worse was to come.

The wider context of this policy of transportation was the fateful appointment in November 1941 of the Head of the SS Secret Police, Reinhard Heydrich as Deputy Protector of Bohemia and Moravia. He was second only to SS Leader Himmler and originator of the policy of the internment and extermination of Jews and others regarded as undesirables. In January 1942 he called a conference at Wannsee near Berlin to discuss the implementation of the policy in the German occupied territories under the disguise of 'resettlement'. He was universally regarded as the coldest of the Nazi leaders of whom even Hitler said: 'The man with the iron heart'.

It was he who ordered the installation of the concentration camp at Theresienstadt, 30 miles north of Prague. Though he set the operations in motion he did not last long. On 27 May 1942 he was assassinated in Prague. The attack was carried out by British trained Czech and Slovak army-in-exile soldiers as part of the resistance. False intelligence in subsequent enquiries led to the name of Lidice, a village just northwest of Prague, being implicated. Consequently, in June the Nazis killed the 340 inhabitants in reprisals, including 88 children. They set the village on fire and razed it to the ground. It was rebuilt in 1949 with a museum, as a monument to the Nazi atrocity.

Terezin

Before the outbreak of war in 1939, Terezin was a small fortress town with a military prison named after the Empress Maria Theresa of Austria when Bohemia was part of the Austro-Hungarian Empire. In 1940 however, the Nazis turned this fortress into Theresienstadt, its German name, which became a large transit concentration camp run by the SS. Despite attempts by the Nazis to sell this camp as a 'safe haven for Jews' away from the ravages of war, it was no such thing. In fact, it was a transit camp and specialised ghetto where it was hoped the inmates would die 'naturally' because of the adverse conditions.

The Schwarz family were transported there from Boskovice on 19 March 1942. Sources vary, but it is commonly recognised that as many as 150,000 to 200,000 Czech Jews including 15,000 children eventually passed through it. Of those, between 90,000 and 97,000 were transported east for 'resettlement', the euphemism the Nazis used to describe the death camps, while 33,000 died there. Of the children at Theresienstadt it estimated that only 150 survived, of whom Lizzy with continuous luck was one.

Theresienstadt Entrance with 'Work Makes You Free' Motto (© Andrew Shiva)

The journey from Brno to Terezin was by cattle train and the Jews were packed as if they actually were cattle into the windowless truck so tightly it was difficult to breath. En-route to the camp Lizzie's father was brutally hit several times by an SS guard because he accidentally knocked over a small lamp standing nearby which he had not seen in the advancing darkness of the evening. This cruel behaviour was regularly the case where any excuse was enough to activate the cruelty of the dreaded SS.

On arrival the town was empty with deserted streets and comprised barrack buildings. Lizzy comments that her mother's heart problem was getting much worse and she developed a 'water swelling condition' in her legs which was painful. The doctor saw her but it kept coming back. She had to be carried there on a stretcher carried by fellow Jews. When they arrived, they were immediately separated, the men from the women going in different directions and her mother was taken to the hospital. Her sister Kitty and herself were put into the women's barracks and during this time Kitty gave the young Lizzy most of her meagre food ration to help curb the endless hunger. The daughters were allowed to visit their mother Hilda once a week but it was difficult for the pair of them to see her like that, declining in health. On one visit to the hospital her mother told them the patients had been visited by two SS men who were asking about which of the patients was the most likely to die. The nurse had identified their mother.

Young Hilda

Meanwhile, her father was interned in the men's barracks and was put in charge of their rations. Shortly afterwards, Lizzy contracted scarlet fever so was in the hospital for six weeks. When she came out from the hospital, she was allowed to visit her mother again. She could not recognise her! She was totally emaciated and her arms had many injection marks and the lower half of her body was very swollen with liquid. After a couple of visits, she died on 14 June 1942. The family were allowed to go to her funeral but it was not really an appropriate experience because there were many others encased in basic wooden coffins without any identification. Sadly, as a result they just could not tell which coffin Hilda's was so were unable to grieve personally.

Lizzy was initially interned with her sister but then Kitty was deported by train on 6 September 1943 to Auschwitz in Poland, on the pretext of helping to build another camp. By this time, they knew that this meant death in the gas chambers. Lizzy said a sad good-bye to her knowing she would almost certainly never see her again unless she was very lucky. Kitty's train took the inmates straight into the gas chamber.

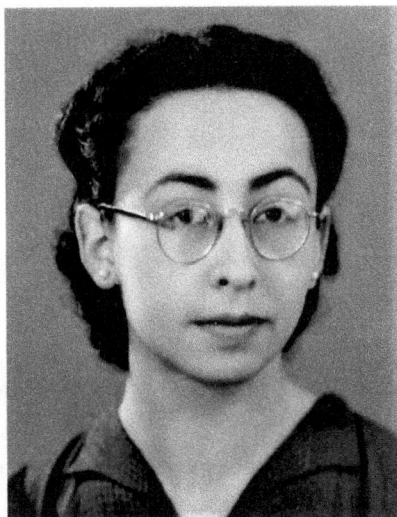

Kitty in 1938

....

JERZY: OFFICER CADET TO PRISONER OF WAR

Jerzy started life in Warsaw in 1920. His father Alfred and his brother Waslav ran a well-known gentleman's outfitter in the city centre which his grandfather Gustav had founded in 1878. By Jerzy's account it had good connections with bespoke tailors in London in the 1930s and their main clients were ministers in the Polish Government and the administration who worked in the historic Royal Castle. Jerzy's mother sadly died when he was two months old. Thereafter he was raised by the housekeeper who his father eventually married in 1926. He got on very well with his stepmother who was a caring woman and a mother to him: "*The mother I knew and loved.*" His adopted brother was eight years his senior and educated in a public school, coming home during vacations. Their life was comfortable until 1933 when he thinks things started to go wrong with the business. On reflection, he does not know why the business started to decline although a possible explanation may have lain in the bigger historical background.

The year 1933 coincided with Hitler becoming Chancellor of Germany and his devious implementation of Nazi Party policies against various ethnic groups at home and abroad. Although there is no direct correlation between the events in Germany and the business in Warsaw, clearly the increasing atmosphere of uncertainty in international business had a negative impact on that trade.

When Jerzy left school in 1938, aged eighteen, he decided to do his compulsory one-year military service immediately: "*To get it out of the way*" he said, before going on to the Warsaw Polytechnic where he hoped to study Engineering. In this year of his entry to the Cadet School, the stability of Central Europe, already threatened by the rise of Nazi Germany was again being forced into another crisis by the trumped-up demands raised by Hitler with reference to Sudetenland in Czechoslovakia.

The result of this for Jerzy and his fellow Officer Cadets was that, in the summer of that year, his unit was mobilised to be updated in modern weapons training and be prepared for any necessary military action. In later life he reflected that, as a young man, he did not really know or care that much about the prevailing international situation but enjoyed the actual training. Also, all the comrades felt confident they would be able to acquit themselves with success in the conflict that appeared to be inevitable.

After the year of training, Jerzy passed his exams and qualified as an Officer Cadet in the Reserve Officers' School of the Polish Army, run by 21/Regiment stationed in Lódź, Eastern Poland. However, with Hitler escalating

European political tension and military intimidation, on completing their year and qualifying ready for release these cadets were kept back in reserve to pass on the training to those who were now being conscripted and to update the older Reservists. He was awarded the rank of Corporal Officer Cadet. "*By the time I passed all the examinations ... the time for my release, the war broke out.*"

The situation deteriorated drastically and quickly. Less than six months after the Munich crisis, in March 1939, Nazi Germany had invaded and occupied zechoslovakia which had clearly always been the second part of that Munich strategy. Later it was discovered that the Mussolini 'paper' had been written by the German Foreign Office, yet another example of Nazi perfidy.

Within another six months Germany invaded Poland on the pretext of an attack by 'Polish troops' who had crossed their border and were shot. These so-called troops were actually concentration camp inmates dressed in Polish uniforms.

There was no delay in action. For the Officer Cadets the war started in earnest that first morning of September at 06.00 hours when Luftwaffe Stuka dive-bombers strafed their regimental barracks dropping bombs causing some casualties. "*We were completely unprepared and we had the diving planes, the so-called Stukas attacking.*" He said the German Army entered their area from the East but must have meant from East Prussia, which was north east of their Lódź garrison.

Their unit was ordered to start out under the command of a General, moving north along the road fully armed with whatever weapons were available but with no mobile units. Thinking they were moving towards the Germans they were in for a very big shock. Instead of meeting the Germans coming in from the north they were met by troops from the Soviet Union coming from an eastern direction.

The back story to this is that whole world had been stunned on 23 August 1939 to learn that Foreign Ministers von Ribbentrop of Nazi Germany and Molotov of the USSR, two nations with diametrically opposed ideologies, had signed a Non-Aggression Pact. What the world did not then know however was, that, hidden beneath this public announcement, both countries had agreed a secret protocol for the shared reorganisation of Eastern Europe when the war started. This involved the partition of Poland between them and the eventual Soviet takeover of the Baltic States of Lithuania, Latvia and Estonia.

This devious, treacherous deal meant that Poland would be divided into separate parts to suit the political and military desires of their more powerful neighbours. So, when Germany invaded Poland from the west on 1 September the focus of the world's attention was on this campaign and while this was going on no one expected that the Soviets would be rolling into eastern Poland on 17 September.

On 28 September, Jerzy and his comrades as part of that unit marching north, without mobile weapons or transport, were confronted by the appearance of the Red Army. Jerzy takes up the story: "*Somehow and I don't know how, we found ourselves between Russian forces from the east and German forces which moved forwards from the west. We were aware that we were between two attacking armies but the danger was from the Germans because they were attacking with everything they had. [] We were very much taken by surprise when the cavalry of strange-looking people started moving around us without fight ... and then we realised they were the Russians and they were not aggressive, supporting us in a way. They surrounded our group and disarmed us which was the natural thing to do.*" The Soviet unit informed the Polish group of about 3,000-4,000 strong that 'the war is finished for you'.

The Soviets marched them towards a small railway siding and loaded them into white truck trains from Russia. The rails had to be assembled in a hurry as they were not the same gauge as was in general use in Poland. After three days they were deep into the Soviet Union first stopping at Kiev in the Ukraine, where they spent a few days in a makeshift camp. The Soviets made lists and conducted the usual military investigations and then they were taken further east to Kharkov, where they were placed in a large proper camp with thousands of other internees.

Jerzy's Warsaw group were further divided into subgroups based on the areas they came from, which was at least a comfort to them. Having had their details checked they were free during the day to pass the time in any way they liked and spent most of the time playing football. They were bored with no interchange of ideas and worse still had no news of how the war was going. Communication was virtually non-existent between the Poles and the Russians as there were considerable language barriers. When asked years later Jerzy said that they never felt threatened as the Russians were not aggressive in any way.

After the organisation into these groups some were told they would eventually be going home in exchange for the people who were now under the Soviet domination of East Poland (Map 3) such as Ukrainians and Jews. Now Jerzy's unit were issued with dry rations and put on a train and told they would be sent back and exchanged with people from the Soviet territory. What they did not know at that time was that Warsaw and Lódź were in the newly occupied German part of Poland.

He was surprised because: "*I was told I would be exchanged with people crossing the Bug river to the Russian part of the Occupation.* (However) *I was directed into the hands of the Germans who immediately formed us into military groups and loaded us onto trains which were waiting.*" This treatment of POWs was not recognised or acceptable under the rules of the Geneva Convention but then the Russians were not signatories. Assured he was going back home to Warsaw Jerzy and comrades found they were in fact going in a very different direction, not West but South!

Nazi-Soviet Divided Poland 1939

JERZY: MIGRANT LABOURER

The next time Jerzy looked out of the train window he saw that they were entering Austria, part of Hitler's Greater Germany since being incorporated by the Nazis in 1938. This was another big concern as to what fate awaited them. They were now interned in a huge POW camp of tens of thousands near Vienna acting as a collection centre where again they were checked, issued with documents before being despatched to various parts of Germany. Strangely, given the Nazi racist ideology of the time, the few military personnel of Jewish origin were treated the same as the Polish Cadet Officers and were also sent to the Officers' camp in uniform. They were in the camp for about a week. At the start they were marched through showers naked, shaved, deloused and their clothes fumigated. On the other side they got their underwear and military uniforms back. They came out processed and clean with typical German precision.

It was not an unusual procedure for them as military personnel but clearly became so later for the Jews of Europe, as Jerzy observed: "*It became very sinister for Jews in concentration camps but was normal for us.*"

This later comment by him was particularly pertinent given that after the war he met his future wife Lizzy

Schwarz in England, who as a Jewish teenager had also been through the same procedure but with fatal results for all her family and most of her fellow inmates. Unlike them she had survived several transits between the major Nazi death camps, against unbelievable odds.

At this camp, the attitude was stricter with periods of regular exercise and walks allowed though always within the clearly demarcated camp fence. They could associate with each other, read magazines, books, play games and so on. They were divided into separate groups with privates in the majority and cadets with the officers. The latter, about 80 strong, were formed into a column and transported by train to an officers' only camp: Oflag VII-A (Offizierslager) at Murnau, in Bavaria very near the Austrian border.

Even though they were in enemy hands it subsequently transpired they were lucky to be POWs in Germany compared to the 8,000 Polish Officers, 6,000 Polish Police and many intellectuals who had remained in Soviet hands and who were subsequently massacred in the Katyn Forest and Kharkov. These assassinations were cold bloodedly carried out in early 1940 on the orders of Beria, Head of the NKVD, the Soviet Internal Security Police.

When this site was discovered in 1943, Stalin, the Soviet dictator, blamed it on the invading Germans from 1941 but later investigations correctly identified the executioners as the Soviets. When the Polish government in exile confronted Stalin he broke off all relations with them and one later consequence of this was Communist government by stealth after the close of the war which prevented the legitimate Polish Government in exile returning from London.

So, although in the hands of the German enemy, unbeknown to them at the time Jerzy and comrades had the first of many strokes of luck by being handed over by the Russians, unlike many of their countrymen later.

What has stuck in Jerzy's memory is an interesting incident on part of that trip. They were in the military column walking into the town when they were ordered to stop. By this time, they had learnt to obey the Germans' instructions immediately for fear of immediate punishment such as the use of rifle butts to beat anyone who did not respond quickly enough.

They were led to the front of a nearby palatial castle. Suddenly a small figure emerged accompanied by two people. It was a General from the old Imperial German Army limping badly with two adjutants beside him. He slowly walked the distance to the column, stood to attention, saluted them and then in broken Polish said: *"I wish the Polish officers more luck in future."* This left a big impression on Jerzy as he noted it was a respectful gesture to the prisoners of war, the epitome of the old Hapsburg Empire: a sharp contrast to the new ruthless Nazis.

In all there were about 250 of them on that train to Murnau and they were issued with rations for the journey. That camp was already filled with Polish officers and had a local commander who negotiated with the German commandant. At this point there was no thought of escape because they were just happy to be finally settled with their own countrymen. There was absolutely no news about how the war was progressing which was frustrating but after a while they realised that a hidden radio had mysteriously appeared in the camp. They were now able to glean some limited information, secretly listening to the BBC broadcasts, soon to be the European Service. This was a very dangerous activity because listening to the BBC had been proscribed by Hitler at the outbreak of war and was punishable by death. In passing, it is interesting to note that this made not the slightest difference to our POWs or to thousands of courageous peoples of the occupied countries during the war who listened regardless to hear the truth as opposed to Nazi propaganda.

However, the news that was leaking through in that winter of 1939-40 was singularly depressing as the war was not going the way they all hoped and prayed for.

This was because by Christmas 1939, Nazi Germany was in control of Austria, incorporated into the Reich in 1938, Czechoslovakia, split into two parts and Western Poland. Britain and France were at war with Germany but still in the phoney war phase as no real conflict seemed to be happening on the western war front, at least on land. This description referred to a strange unreal period where the combatants were engaged in a stand-off. Clearly this situation had a big effect on the morale of the POWs. Apart from the incessant bad news that occasionally filtered through, life in the camp was well organised with cultural activities, such as music, lectures, seminars and these were used to assess life in Poland before the war, the politics and why the sudden defeat had happened. They received regular mail and Jerzy had contact from his elder brother in Warsaw who had been invalided out of the military a long time ago and was telling him that the family members were safe.

They were kept in this camp about six months including the Christmas period. The food was judged to be passable but inadequate, especially for young men in the prime of life. Breakfasts were a slice of dreadful bread with margarine and coffee, lunches comprised the bread again and a ghastly watery soup made mostly from swede, also known as yellow turnip. From that day onwards Jerzy said he hated that vegetable with a vengeance! Dinner, if it could be called such, was often some kind of greasy ersatz sausage with margarine. They were given a quarter of a loaf every day. Jerzy said he had never been so hungry in all his life.

The daily routine common to all camps was to rise at 07.00 hours to be on parade at 08.00 hours for counting. After that ritual they were free to move around a big area and receive parcels from home, although this did not work at all well because there seemed to be very few. They were also under pressure from the Polish commanders to keep fit and not fall sick although most had to attend the sick bay at least a couple of times. Obviously, the keeping fit ritual was part of the military training in case they were called into action in any way again. When in the sick bay Jerzy had some of his blood taken for research every two to three days and understandably found this very unpleasant. *"At that camp there was a Doctor Kusch, who based his medical activity on a water treatment ... horrific sometimes. Actually, his name was known worldwide [...] involving immersion in hot then suddenly extreme cold water directed at us."* The extreme shock apparently produced some positive results.

The year 1940 bore yet more bad news. At 04.15 hours on 9 April the Germans suddenly invaded Denmark overrunning the country in six hours. This was the lightning war or Blitzkrieg, already employed against Poland, a concentrated combination of rapid powerful motorised and armoured attacks supported by air in the West which left the enemy totally disorganised. The real objective was neutral Norway which was strategically important for shipping out Swedish iron ore from one of its ports and because the German navy could operate better in the Atlantic. However, the Norwegians proved to be a tougher proposition lasting out for over two months before being totally defeated and occupied. The German excuse was to protect them from the British who, with the French, came to their aid.

However, during this campaign, the Germans invaded the Netherlands, Belgium, Luxemburg and France on 10 May using Blitzkrieg tactics. The Dutch army lasted six days while the Belgians held out for three weeks.

The battle for France was over in six weeks, the German Army having outwitted the French and British by attacking through the Ardennes, thus bypassing the Maginot line believed to be virtually impregnable.

Consequently, the Polish POWs began to see an enormous influx of Dutch, Belgian and French inmates. Although separated from them by a wire fence, they were nevertheless able to communicate and to catch up on the war news which was even worse than hitherto imagined.

The Nazis now dominated all of mainland Europe except Switzerland, which was neutral along with Spain and Portugal, Britain's oldest ally. Spain, although technically neutral, was sympathetic to the Nazis having been subject to a fascist coup by General Franco in the Spanish Civil War.

The map shows the development of Nazi Germany's conquest and occupation of Europe by December 1940, numbered in order of the events, as they occurred:

1. Remilitarisation of the Rhineland, 7 March 1936.

2. Annexation of Austria into 'Greater Germany', 12 March 1938. 3. Sudetenland, 1 October 1938.

4. Czechoslovakia, 15 March 1939: Bohemia-Moravia Protectorate and Slovak Republic (German satellite).

5. Poland, 1 September 1939, Nazi-Soviet partition, 9 October 1939.

Western Blitzkrieg 1940: 6. Denmark, 9 April. 7. Norway, 9 April -10 June. 8. Netherlands, 10 - 17 May.

9. Luxembourg, 10 May. 10. Belgium, 10 - 18 May. 11. France, 10 May – 22 June.

In France, the whole coast was protected by a formidable and intimidating array of defences known as the Atlantic Wall. Between June 1940, after the fall of France, the air born Battle of Britain that summer and the subsequent devastating night-time raids of the winter Blitz, and June 1941when the Nazis reneged on the pact with the Soviet Union by invading it, only Britain stood alone against them.

At this point it seemed that the whole of European civilisation was being obliterated by the repulsive Nazi policy of racism and destruction of anyone or anything that existed in opposition to their extreme beliefs.

In the Nazi state and in their occupied territories the vanquished people were categorised based on racial identity. Everyone except the Aryan race of Nordic origin was considered to belong to 'out-groups'.

However, there were gradations in the system. At the top of this tree were the similar racial groups of Sweden, Denmark, Norway and Holland, the last three now occupied. Below them were all those of Slavic origin particularly the Poles and Russians who were considered culturally and physically inferior.

At the very bottom of this human pile were the Jews who were continually persecuted from the moment the Nazis came to power in 1933 along with Gypsies, Roma and Sinta considered to be racially defective.

December 1940

German Occupied Europe, December 1940

Shortly after their stay in Murnau, the POWs were sent off to what was called a 'punishment camp' in the eastern area of North Holland. This was to instil discipline. They had to sleep on a floor covered with straw, in damp conditions which Jerzy since said *"characterised the whole area"*. The Germans made them work in fields digging up peat, in strong boots but with no special weatherproof clothes. Officer POWS, as Jerzy and his unit were, should never have been used as forced labour under the terms of the Geneva Convention but this clearly did not apply to Poles because the Nazis despised them as an inferior species.

In their work camp in Holland the Polish POWs, continued to receive food, which was poor but adequate, combined with tough discipline, as every command had to be carried out immediately or else there were severe consequences. The worst thing was the frequent invasions of the barracks at 2 or 3am during which they were made to stand up to be counted as well as taunted depending on how well behaved they had been. The duration of this interruption to sleep could be short, medium or very long based on how cooperative they had been as judged by the camp guards: clearly an early example of psychological torture.

After a year of being in this camp some prisoners started to escape but were always caught. The others had to stand and to watch as the recently caught escapees were sent along a corridor of soldiers while they were hit and kicked as punishment, before being taken off to solitary confinement to reinforce discipline and discourage further escape attempts. On the other hand, cultural life was acceptable particularly as there was one among them who was a university lecturer. The cadets were now allowed to organise lectures, discussions and other educational activities and to start a theatre group which put on reviews.

"*In that respect*", observed Jerzy, "*the German guards were helpful, even providing some costumes for the shows. However, we were not allowed to mix with the other nationalities as each group was confined by wire netting which no one was allowed near.*"

In 1941, the group was sent away to another POW camp, Stalag VI/G at Hoffnungsthall, about 15 miles from the centre of Cologne. Jerzy said it was a military area where the forces carried out manoeuvres. They were still in their original uniforms. From their camp near Cologne they were sent all over the country in small groups to bolster the increasing shortages in the workforce which demonstrated the decrease of available manpower as the war wore on. Initially, over 1.5 million POWs were commandeered to cover for the shortages. After 1943, over 5 million civilians of all nationalities were forced into slave labour, mostly in the Nazi homeland. Jerzy's fellow POWs were typical of many Poles in the early days of the war who were brought in to be farm workers without any pay.

In 1942, 3,000 of them were still together there and they witnessed the devastating bombing of Cologne. "*It was very spectacular at night of course mostly by American planes (*) and we were excited as it seemed the war was shifting away from the Germans. At one point the camp was hit by a low flying plane which started firing at the barracks and sadly one of the POWs was killed in this raid. Cologne had dreadful raids at night ... very ... very huge raids.*" (* It was the Royal Air Force who did night-time bombing in 1942, while the Americans flew daylight sorties.)

After being sometime in the camp near Cologne, about 70 of them were sent to another camp, Oflag VI/H, in a place called Rothe Erder, a heavy industrial centre, a district in east Aachen which was adjacent to some railway sidings where there was a warehouse. Their job was unloading trains to put goods off the trains in the warehouse for future use: hay for the cavalry, military uniforms, occasionally food and wines from France and frozen food, which they saw as a blessing. Naturally, some of this: *"fell off the back of a lorry ... it always did!"* English humour years later.

They were being moved about all over Germany because as the war progressed the Nazis had serious workforce problems and increasingly had to rely on forced foreign labour. Ironically, it was this very work and the unintentional help from their guards that eventually gave them the opportunity for their escape. Jerzy and his three close friends had always considered escaping from a camp and had been talking about it for a long time. What they needed was a good opportunity. They decided that when such an opportunity presented itself, they should be ready to go. They now realised that, because of the way they worked near to the perimeter of

Polish POWs unloading hay

Hoffnungsthal, 16 April 1942, Jerzy second row, far right

Aachen 1942, (Note the guard with a walking stick!)

the railway sidings, this could be their best chance. Not only that, but Aachen was very close to the Belgian border which would increase their chance of hiding amongst a less hostile population people who resented the occupation. They began to set things in motion and awaited the next best opportunity.

As seen, the paranoid Nazi racist ideology fell harder on the Jews seen to be Bolshevik plotters against the survival of Germany. This bizarre ideology did not sit well officially with their recently acquired Bolshevik ally, the USSR in 1939 but both sides were benefitting politically so expediency ruled. Historical hindsight has however shown that, despite their conflicting ideologies, the treatment and methods in their relative zones of occupation was strikingly similar in its terror to groups considered racially inferior.

This realpolitik was blown asunder when the Germans invaded the Soviet Union in 1941. The Nazis extended their torture, mass death and systematic extermination of the *Untermensch* (inferior people) to the Russian zone of Poland and in the Eastern part of Russia as part of their policy of creating living space for their own people. This was perpetrated by the Einstatzgruppen (Task Force, namely mobile killing squads) of the Schutzstaffel (SS). Thousands upon thousands of Jews, Roma, Slavs and Communist Commissars attached to each Red Army unit were liquidated. Initially welcomed by the Ukrainians who saw the German Army as liberators from communist repression their murderous behaviour soon backfired and resulted in fierce partisan resistance. Any captured prisoners from either side were killed immediately without a second thought.

In Germany, the increasing scope of this mass transportation and murder of the Jews ironically aided our comrades in their escape plans with fortuitous consequences for their future. One of their previous jobs in the town had been clearing out the houses compulsorily vacated by the Jews being transported to the concentration camps.

Back in Aachen, in those empty houses by sheer chance they got hold of some boiler suits as well as some maps of the surrounding area which would prove invaluable. They still needed money to get from Belgium through to France, so they traded their Red Cross cigarettes and coffee for the 'stiff currency' of Reichsmarks with their guards, with whom they had an amicable relationship. One of the inmates made a compass from a razor blade and magnetised it. When placed in water this 'compass' would swing around and finally point to the magnetic north. This was to be a crucial tool for any escape plan which involved travelling over many miles without being able to easily check official directions.

Jerzy and his close friends Gustav, Adrian, a student and Lugwig, an older man, rehearsed an escape plan remaining alert to any opportunity presented by the train unloading. All their fellow inmates knew this and agreed to help them in any way they could.

....

ESCAPE!

Then, out of the blue, came the very thing they were hoping and waiting for. A train had come in under darkness and needed urgent unloading in three hours. They were called out in the middle of the night to do the job. It was 2 October 1942. Away from the platform inside the storage bunkers it was very dark, almost black and with little background light. There were too few guards on duty and everyone was concentrating on the rapid unloading of the train under subdued light.

This was it! It was a heaven-sent opportunity and they agreed they would never get a better chance. The other thirty or so POWS unloading in the work detail were 'in' on the plan and agreed to cover for them, for as long as it was realistic possible. With their boiler suits under their army uniforms and only some dry biscuits for food, their maps and the homemade compass, they stealthily slipped off to the boundary fence. With some difficulty and in danger of being seen by the guards any second, they climbed over it. With their hearts in their mouths they sneaked away into the pitch blackness beyond. "*It was very easy*" Jerzy said. Despite his understatement years after the event it surely cannot have been as easy as he said. There was always the risk of getting snagged on the fence and of failure. However, they were the first to escape at night which made them proud. It was 2am.

Splitting into two pairs to avoid too much suspicion they set off surreptitiously into the town as directed by the map. Their aim was the border with nearby Belgium. After a while Jerzy and Adrian heard footsteps following them. They quickened their pace but still the footsteps were there. Thinking they were discovered they quickly hid in the bushes near the road, dreading the outcome. When the footsteps came along side of them, it was the other pair! By then they were outside the town and in the countryside.

Now out in the surrounding countryside some light thrown by the moon in between the clouds was visible. On the one hand this helped them see their way around but, on the other, raised the problem of being seen outside in the curfew period and as strangers to the locality. Despite this threat they kept to the road as much as possible using the self-made compass to direct them but always ready to dive into the undergrowth if they ran into a German patrol or, for that matter, anyone. Rothe Erde is East of Aachen so it took a couple of perilous hours to make their way from the railway siding there around the outskirts of the town in the countryside and carry onto the Belgian border, a trek of about six miles.

They walked nonstop until four in the morning and then with the dawn approaching climbed a very steep hill overlooking the whole area. Here they spent the whole day secluded in the bushes and sleeping as much as they could. They felt safe on this hill with a good view of the whole landscape and the road below. When darkness came, they set off again back down and continued mainly close to the road.

They were elated and excited as they made their way on foot. "*We were certainly very high for at least two nights.*" With a strict curfew in place they had to stay super alert to any human activity to avoid attracting any attention from the only people allowed out, namely the authorities. Also, given the deficiencies of their camp diet it was a tiring trek so not surprising that progress became slower. Existing only on their dry biscuits and some fruit picked from trees in the fields they followed their homemade compass and eventually they came to a crossroads where there was a stone signpost. It was in French! "*We knew that we were in Belgium.*" They continued through large fruit plantations avoiding any houses but feasting on all the fruit. Their only company was the cows in the fields which kept coming inquisitively up to them, much to their irritation.

In the early morning they knew they were in the southern French-speaking part of the country because somebody with a flickering light approached them. It was a farmer out for the early morning milking and he addressed them in French. Adrian, who spoke French, said they were POWs. The farmer told them that there were a lot of German patrols in the area coming along the roads. He explained where the best place was to cross the road to avoid bumping into these patrols. Fortunately, the road was very narrow to cross so they would not be in the open too long. On the other side was some artificial fencing over which the farmer said was "pure Belgium". They crossed the road one by one.

What this farmer's phrase exactly meant is unclear, but it strongly suggests that perhaps they had not quite crossed the border into the French-speaking part of Belgium itself but were actually very close to it but had wandered across into Holland. Historically Belgium was part of the Netherlands Kingdom until 1830 when it became independent. Aachen is adjacent to both Holland and Belgium and therefore shares a common border with both. Also, this whole area is one that in the Holy Roman Empire was part of modern France and Germany which had shared culture and languages, a characteristic of all border areas. The stone sign in French may have dated back to the period when Aachen was called Aix-la-Chapelle in French and which was the coronation site of the famous Holy Roman Emperor Charlemagne. This confusion was understandable because it seemed that this narrow road was in fact straddling the border, so they may have been across it back and forth a couple of times. Nevertheless, they were pleased to be informed they had reached Belgium. The first phase of their plan had been successful. Goodbye Germany.

It was now mid-morning on Saturday 3 October, so they carried on to the next farm and met another helpful farmer. He directed them to the local doctor in the village who also happened to be the organiser for the local underground. Another stroke of fortune! The doctor welcomed them openly and they spent quite some time there undercover, eating good food after days of hunger. *"We introduced ourselves. We spent quite a lot of time during the day eating proper food to keep going. He took all our details to pass on ... we had been given vague addresses and where to look for help. The next aim was Liège."* Jerzy wanted to rest there awhile but the others wanted to press on to the next stop. They were right because in this precarious situation it was imperative to keep on the move. The doctor gave them information, directions and addresses where to call and get help.

While they were being well looked after they thought how compassionate and brave these people were because helping them was literally a matter of life and death. If any civilians were caught helping enemies of the state they would almost certainly be tortured for information, followed by certain death at the hands of the dreaded Gestapo.

They followed the directions walking to their next destination, which was Liège, about 5 kilometres or so and on arriving there it was 7 o'clock in the evening. The city centre was teeming with German soldiers. Immediately there was a problem. The address they had been given had been written down mistakenly. Misery and panic set in. What were they to do now? There they were in a strange city with no friendly contact. *"It was a Saturday"* said Jerzy which meant they had been walking on and off all that day and were dog tired. Darkness was setting in and they began to realise that they were in big trouble as they were outdoors without any hiding place in the city and this was the curfew hour.

Being in a city in daylight with many people about was always a very tense situation for fear of discovery or, worse still, betrayal. Being there as darkness fell and at the start of a curfew was even more precarious. Then yet again they had a bit more luck. As darkness fell, a woman with a young daughter appeared before them. They asked her what time the curfew began. "*Why do you want to know?*" she asked. In sheer desperation they took a chance hoping against hope she would not report them. "*We're escaping POWs,*" they said. This was a blind and dangerous leap of faith for she could have been anyone, possibly a collaborator or at least someone not wanting to become involved. Instead she said: "*It starts right now*". Then, in a bizarre twist, she and her daughter spoke to them in broken Polish. What relief and what a coincidence! It transpired that she was the laundress for the local Gestapo. She took them back to her house which even more coincidentally was right next door to Gestapo Headquarters in the city. They could not believe their eyes. Another lucky escape! The comrades stayed secreted over Sunday in her loft right next to the enemy's secret police. Imagine what must have gone through their minds. In a severely restricted space, they were stuck in the shallow attic too close to the partition dividing them from the Gestapo headquarters with the worse kind of Germans just feet away below them. They were cramped by not being able to move about much and could not speak other than in the quietest whisper for 24 hours, a big challenge carrying dangerous consequences.

Provided they remained still and quiet, no one would have thought to look for them there. They could not travel in their boiler suits on a Sunday which would clearly have aroused suspicions.

The brave Liège 'laundress', left and daughters

What a wonderful and brave woman, thought Jerzy. They never got her name nor knew how much she was involved in the underground. Of course, later they realised this was all most probably part of the escapee trail strategy, that all members in this chain had false names and only knew those they worked closely with on what is called 'a need to know basis'. This was so that under interrogation they could not give away their comrades.

While they were there, the woman explored the possibility of getting the desperate POWs out of the country quickly by plane, using a route through which many downed pilots were transported back to Britain. Unfortunately, this could not be arranged immediately for such a small group.

They had to be moved on quickly though, another necessary part of this movement of POWs and air crews, for to be in one place too long without proper identity papers was to invite suspicion and interrogation, with the likely consequences.

There was an alternative route used by many others hunted by the Germans, so it was agreed they would move on to a safe address in Lille. This was that of a dentist and his daughter who had previously corresponded with one of them in the POW camp previously. They were accompanied by a woman who took them on the tram to Lille and whom they had to follow at a discreet distance whilst she got the tickets and she travelled slightly removed from them to their next destination right to the address in Lille.

All this activity was a surprise to them. Clearly, there was a whole undercover organisation whose existence was purely to frustrate the Germans by arranging escape routes back to England via Spain. This situation *"caused us much fright"* said Jerzy because any error in the chain or in any public arena, for example unwittingly saying something in one's native language, however slight, might result in disaster. Any family helping escapees was in extreme danger if discovered. It would be the end of anyone concerned and often was widened to include other innocent parties by association. The Germans were ruthless and callously cruel to anyone who opposed them. Nevertheless, in the face of this they were incredibly courageous people.

Most of their travelling had been done after dark through countryside, both by their choice to avoid being seen or by other people's instructions to avoid attracting unnecessary attention causing problems. This made obvious sense because at night they would be able to operate largely unseen although, by the same token in curfew hours with no locals out, being observed outside was to invite immediate trouble. Either way, their trail through these various points of contact was hazardous every step of the way.

That day they hid in the dentist's large office in the garden for that very reason. Despite the very real danger the family were welcoming and looked after them well. When the time was right towards the evening the dentist's daughter took them to the railway station and bought their tickets to their next destination: Amiens.

Still with no proper official recognised papers, except military documents, they embarked by train to Amiens. The carriage was very empty which was fortunate in that no one would be around to talk to them. Nevertheless, it could spell danger if they stood out from their very few fellow passengers during any possible troop inspections. They continued to travel in separate pairs to avoid attracting too much attention. They still had their boiler suits from before on over their uniforms. The journey took about an hour and a half.

At Amiens they had an address to go to but when they arrived there it proved to be a false lead. Since it was around midnight, they quickly left the town and went into the countryside to hide. They called at a nearby farm but the family would not open the door to them, so they had to sleep in a field. Here they were exposed to danger with no safe house, stuck out in the countryside and hoping they were not seen. Faced with a dead end, Jerzy took control and decided they should move on urgently so the next day they went back to the station and bought tickets for Paris. They had a French friend there from the Medical Corps who had been in a POW camp with them earlier in the war and when released had left his address for them to call on him in an emergency. This was undoubtedly an emergency.

They arrived in Paris in the afternoon and immediately encountered many German soldiers who were using the city for relaxation and recreation when on leave from operations. The city was bustling with people, so luckily, they were able to lose themselves in the crowds milling around near the centre. They found the address they had been given in the city centre but the Frenchman was not at home, so they had to wait. This was an anxious time as even discreet loitering could have exposed them to a challenge to show their papers by the French police or a German soldier at any time. To avoid this possibility, they split up and spread out for the time being and tried to avoid attracting any unnecessary attention. This was a potentially dangerous situation. Eventually their French friend appeared and with a sigh of relief they were safe again. He put them up in a little hotel for the night, with no names asked for.

He got them tickets for the next day to Lyon. However, the only problem was that the city was in Vichy France in the so-called Unoccupied Zone. This would however involve crossing the border at the historic town of Moulins, which was the original capital of the Bourbon family whose descendants were the royal family of France until the revolution. Now it was the heavily guarded border post between the German Occupied Zone and the Vichy French Unoccupied Zone and this meant document inspection would be standard procedure.

The history of the establishment of this zone was that, after the German Blitzkrieg in the west through Holland, Belgium and France, a badly beaten France surrendered to the Germans on 17 June 1940. The Franco-German Armistice was signed between them on 22 June. Under this arrangement, the French army was to be completely disbanded and Germany occupied two thirds of the country and all along the coastline (Map). The remaining third in the southern part of the country was technically unoccupied and governed by a puppet government. This new French government was headed by the aged Marshal Phillipe Pétain, ironically the national hero of the successful defence of Verdun in 1916 but now humbled into collaborating with the Nazis. It was known as the Vichy Régime, after the town in the centre of France which became the ipso facto capital of this subject state.

Divided France 1940

German ally Italy also gained a small piece of territory in the south east. In September, Germany, Italy and Japan signed an agreement in Berlin known as the Axis. During this period over 2 million French soldiers were kept captive in Germany and used as forced labour.

On the journey, they were in continuous danger of being caught but miraculously no one asked for their papers but just the tickets, enabling a simple non-threatening and non-verbal interaction. As they did not have the required documents, they had been instructed by their French friend to get off at the previous station to enable a night-time crossing on foot.

....

DANGER AT THE LINE

October 1942 in the middle of France. The four Polish escapee Prisoners of War (POWs) are on a train approaching Moulins, the city on the demarcation line between the German Occupied and the Unoccupied Zones of France. They are Jerzy Dyszkiewicz, Adrian Sosenkowski, Gustav Kubrit and Ludwig Hermanowski, all Cadet Officers in the Polish Army. They have escaped from a POW camp near Aachen close to the Belgian-German border. They are disguised in boiler suits over their army uniforms and have covertly negotiated a tenuous passage through Belgium and France to finally reach this point of relative safety from discovery and capture.

They are on the train from Paris where resistance contacts there have arranged tickets for them to take a train to Lyon, an ancient city in the eastern central part of the country. However, this poses a serious problem for them as the city is located well within the Unoccupied Zone. They do not have the required papers to enter officially. In fact, very few people were issued with them. This is an unsurmountable barrier to their bid of making it to freedom. To bypass this, their Paris contact has told them to get off at the stop just before the actual frontier. This stop is less policed so reduces the inevitable inspection of official papers. Later, the intention is to find their way through the countryside with a guide and cross over into the Unoccupied Zone after dark. and continue their journey relatively unnoticed and untroubled in their goal to reach neutral Spain.

Travelling in pairs and sitting well apart to avoid attracting any undue attention from other passengers they are trying hard to conceal their natural apprehension yet are inwardly excited at reaching this final stage in their journey to freedom after what has been a perilous but lucky journey. Strangely, at every point on this tense journey whenever they were in danger of discovery and certain capture, they have been surprised that something or someone has turned up seemingly on cue to rescue them.

As their stop approaches, they stand up ready to alight but the train speeds through their station. This is an absolute disaster. The next station is Moulins which is right on the line between the two parts of the divided France.

Standard procedure is that all passengers will have to get down off the train onto the platform to have their papers checked before travelling onwards. Without papers all will be lost. How will they get around this challenge and save themselves? Without the required documents and given their civilian disguises they will immediately be seized by the authorities and subjected to severe interrogation and almost certain death as spies.

Our central character, Jerzy, takes up the story. He noticed that the station was filled with German border guards, troops and police: "*We had no hope of getting out of there*" he later said.

What happened next came as a complete surprise to him. "*Suddenly the one who was the most nervous one came down across the track and we followed. We crossed to the other side. We came up on the platform where the German troops were.*" In their boiler suits the Germans ignored them thinking they were railway workers attending to the track. This quick thinking by the oldest, the one they thought least likely to act spontaneously, had the desired effect. Without anyone noticing them a real French railwayman appeared and urgently muttered: "Hello, hello, suivez moi!" In a flash, he recognised what was going on. Without any hesitation they followed him and within a couple of minutes they were in a crowded street in the town centre and out of sight in the large crowd. "*We just didn't believe what happened but we were not yet in the unoccupied zone but still in the town on the occupied side.*" However, it was an amazing fortuitous moment never to be forgotten. Right under the very noses of the troops and police checking everything and everybody, thanks to some lightning thinking, they had just assumed the identity of 'railway workers' extricating themselves from a dangerous situation without even a passing glance.

Close to freedom and yet still in the German zone they would still have to find somewhere to stay out of sight until night. While doing this, the next move suddenly happened to them for they met a 'lady of the night', as later described. The railwayman told her who they were. Without hesitation, she too motioned to them surreptitiously: "*Suivez moi*" and they followed her to a charity kitchen where they spent the rest of the day hiding among the cabbages and other vegetables! They had to be very careful not to be seen but they did try to help things out a bit here and there with the preparing of food as best they could. The person in charge of the kitchen knew they were POWs but their secret was safe with him.

Later, the 'lady of the night' arranged for them to meet a young Frenchman who would lead them across the border into the Unoccupied Zone that night. Under cover of darkness they followed 50 yards behind this brave young Frenchman and towards the Allier River right on the frontier. He wished them: "*Bon chance! Bon chance! Vive la France Libre!*" and they jumped chest high into the water. Jerzy recalls it was freezing but they were so excited they did not even feel it. They thrashed their way across this fast-flowing river with increasing relief to be away from the constant danger that had accompanied them throughout this journey. The Frenchman waited until they were safely across on to the opposite bank and waved them farewell through the trees. They waved back to him in gratitude, soaking wet but deliriously happy. Now they were in Vichy France, that part of the country which was not technically occupied by the Germans. For our escapees this now meant that they were relatively free and untroubled although there was now an urgent need to obtain some form of approved civilian identification.

Drying off, they walked to a nearby farm and were thankfully put up by a local farmer for the night. It was a Saturday night they will remember forever.

They ate a much-appreciated meal of French bread, cheese and drank red wine. The cheese particularly left a big impression on Jerzy and he remembered it as Roquefort and loved it for the rest of his life. This simple meal, after their ongoing lack of proper food on their long fraught journey, *"was a nothing short of fantastic feast"*, as Jerzy described it. As they reflected on their run of luck that brought them here, they could relax for a short time and they fell into a deep sleep. Having arrived in Vichy France during October 1942, 22-year old Jerzy and his compatriots had been the beneficiaries of an incredible run of luck.

The overnight stay at the farm in Vichy France, gave them an opportunity to take stock about their journey so far. Reflecting on his experiences after the war, Jerzy recalled that at that point: *"We were in Free France"*. However, this was a misnomer as, although this zone was known as *zone libre* as opposed to *zone occupé,* the idea of being free here was not strictly accurate other than in colloquial parlance. The word 'libre' represented a complete charade since this state operated under the close eye of the conquering Germans and the collaborationist police. It is understandable that Jerzy thought this because of the way the zone was referred to.

In fact, this travesty was in stark contrast to the exiled self-titled *Free French* constituted after the disaster of 1940 who continued the fight for the allies under General de Gaulle, stationed in London. Whilst the comrades considered themselves to be free, in the true sense of the word they were far from it. Freedom was neither the case for the 75,000 Jews who were rounded up and deported to the death camps so enthusiastically by the Vichy Police and the paramilitary Milice, that even some of the SS were taken aback by their racist zeal.

In the escape they had been constantly heartened by these seemingly ordinary people who were prepared to take extreme risks and put them up without any question. They marvelled at these civilians who were a vital part of the secret war against the occupiers but who showed such courage risking everything by putting their and their families' lives at risk of certain torture and death. They concluded they must either hate the occupiers or possibly be part of an informal chain in the underground resistance. Most of the population implicitly resented the occupation but many were prepared to act. This was demonstrated when the farmer gave them a much-needed change of underwear and told them what to do for the next stage. They would have to get on the train and say who they were. This strangely resulted in them not having to pay as the tickets were already booked for the next stop of Auch.

After their overnight stay in Moulins, with the farmer and the memorable meal, it now became obvious that the escape route would have to be a southern one via Spain. This would entail an extremely tough trek along what was known as 'The Freedom Trail', across the peaks of the Pyrenees, the mountains straddling France and Spain. These were a collection of routes used by

British and American air crews and many civilians fleeing the Nazis. First though, they had to negotiate the route there. The farmer who gave them their last meal had told them what to do and where to go next.

They had spent one night with the farmer and the next night they had slept in a hayloft. Jerzy and his comrades continued to marvel at this network of people who took such great risks to confound the hated occupiers.

The next part of the journey was having to take a train to Auch which was the covert: "*centre for the administration*" (of the Polish military). As planned, they said who they were and did not have to pay the fare. This centre was one of many helping to hide escapees and to send them onwards. There they were required to adopt a new identity being issued with the relevant papers saying they had completed their service and had been demobilised from the French Army. This was a cover for their situation as, after the defeat in 1940, the French Army was demobilised so no longer considered an active organisation. They were given a French demobilisation kit of new civilian clothes, some money and tickets to the south of France where there was another Polish centre in the Ariège Region, close to the border with Andorra.

Jerzy and his friends now had the required papers but in their Polish names. This was clearly a ruse to disguise their real identities, for although technically free, there were potential problems that could still arise even in this zone as the puppet administration was still in hock to their Nazi masters. Adrian spoke French, so he provided good cover for them.

The context of this arrangement was that, after the defeat and partition of Poland by Germany and the Soviet Union in October 1939, over 200,000 able bodied men managed to escape by various circuitous routes and ended up in Britain and France, forming the Polish army-in-exile under General Sikorski. In France the numbers rose from 1,900 in 1939 and rose to 84, 461 in 1940. Many others operated in different resistance movements in France after the armistice in June 1940, hence this centre in Auch.

When later asked, Jerzy said he did not know what happened to the boiler suits but now they were in civilian clothes, reasonable ones at that, which were part of the subterfuge. They had money, not much, but enough and tickets to the South of France where there was another Polish 'centre' in Aulus-les-Bains, near Tarascon in the Ariège Region of the Midi-Pyrenees.

There were now about 30 of them in that centre officially waiting for visas for America for eventual use in Spain. However, Germany was at now war with the United States. In fact, this was a cover story as they were waiting to be taken from Spain to Gibraltar then landed in Britain. So, whilst waiting there the comrades relaxed and began to think ahead to what life would be like in a new country.

Looking back, their journey through Belgium and France (Map) had been amazingly lucky in that they were never seriously challenged by the authorities and on two occasions swift heart-in-the mouth thinking had extricated them from danger.

Escape Journey 1942

· · · · · · · ·

LIZZY IN THE CAMPS

On the same day that Jerzy and his comrades were escaping, over 700 miles to the East, Lizzy Schwarz, a fifteen-year old Jew was not sharing any such luck. She had been incarcerated with her elder sister and father in Theresienstadt Concentration camp, north of Prague, since being transported in March, travelling in overcrowded windowless cattle trucks and was now existing and working on a starvation diet in hellish conditions. Lizzy's sister Kitty, seven years older than her, continually gave much of her bigger ration to her, a truly selfless act in those terrible conditions. Her mother Hilda had died in that June from long-term complications of a heart condition in a camp hospital clearly exacerbated by the cruel treatment meted out to anyone who was not able to remain fit to work.

Her father Moric was detained in a separate section of the camp and the daughters were only allowed to meet him when given permission for two visits to their dying mother, once in hospital and then when attending her funeral at a makeshift cemetery of unnamed wooden coffins. During the following year the inevitable happened, Lizzy's sister was taken away to Auschwitz 'to help build another camp' a euphemism for the gas chamber. The Nazis were always very adept at fooling everybody about their intentions and their actions both from their victims to those in the outside world. Saying goodbye was extremely painful for Lizzy because it was now being rumoured that this was one of the many death camps and Lizzy felt she would likely never see Kitty again. Rumours about the death camps were already beginning to spread among those being transported.

At this point though, despite sadly losing her elder sister in the worst of circumstances, Lizzy's luck was in because she was considered too young to go to Auschwitz, being fit enough to take on the grinding workload expected from those who were still being kept alive. However, on top of that she had another break, if it can be called that, because she contracted typhoid fever, a rapidly spreading disease caused by unclean water and food. She was hospitalised for six weeks, a brief respite from the endless routine. Once out of hospital there was no question of a recuperation period in these harsh conditions but straight back to backbreaking work on a starvation diet. Later, she also contracted Encephalitis also known to her as 'sleeping sickness. Given the general attitude of the Nazis to the ill and infirm in those camp conditions, whereby they were regarded as of no further use therefore dispensable, it seems clear that it was the young and able who were considered more useful for future work. Thus, Lizzy's illness ironically worked in her favour, the first in a series of lucky breaks in the dreaded selection process of the SS camp guards.

Without any access to her father, in the separate barracks for the men, she was now totally isolated with no family contact. Here was a stark contrast to her earlier idyllic rural existence in the hills around Boskovice.

Without direct experience of these camps one can only struggle to imagine what it was like in these inhuman filthy disease-ridden conditions as a lonely teenager.

Photos and films about the killing camps can never capture the full horror of the inmate's daily existence. They may portray disgusting unimaginable conditions but these are obviously viewed by the audience second-hand. Real-life was much worse. The inmates were kept barely above survival conditions, merely existing in untold filth and kept alive to do the continual backbreaking manual work required by the Nazi system or to be left to die if they could not. Disease was rampant and highly infectious and contagious sweeping through a block or the camp with frightening speed. The rations were the bare minimum and they resorted to eating whatever that could grab to supplement them. Any attempt to do this would incur cruel summary punishment. They were sleeping, often three in a row, in overcrowded single infested bunks and continually afraid that there would be a call out at a moment's notice to line up and be selected for a trip to 'work' in another camp which, by now, meant certain death on arrival. In Theresienstadt one was continually subject to a form of Russian roulette, only one selection queue away from the killing camp of Auschwitz-Birkenau.

After the enforced departure of Kitty, totally alone and missing the older sister who had looked after her and clearly been a comfort to her, Lizzy spent a year in that camp. She was living in a block which had one family to one bunk bed, regardless of numbers. During the day the inmates grew vegetables and, when they could get away with it, they secreted some in their rags and took them back to eat. On that detail she often stole tomatoes hiding them in her clothes to help with the inadequate food. She said that they were always hungry.

Somewhat surprisingly, later in life, Lizzy described her experiences of the dreadful conditions in the concentration camps in a seemingly matter of fact way that clearly disguised the deep emotions felt at that time. She was a vulnerable teenager on her own fearing for her life and on a daily or minute by minute basis. She has most likely consigned this to the deep recesses of her mind to enable her to engage with life after the war and beyond.

The only interruption to this ghastly ritual came on 23 June 1944 just 17 days after the D Day landings on the Normandy coast by the Allies. This event has entered the historical annals as a famous hoodwinking exercise by the Nazi authorities. There was an inspection of the camp by two Swiss Representatives of the International Red Cross and two Danish Representatives. This was because over 450 Danish Jews had been transferred there in late 1943 and the Danish and the neutral Swedish leaders insisted on an inspection. At this point of the war, Hitler needed the Danes to be kept compliant because of their vital contribution to the workforce and had to keep the neutral Swedes on board to continue the supply of vital war materiel, particularly large amounts of iron ore.

The Nazis were also now concerned about the eventual outcome of the war as Germany was being attacked from all sides: in the east by the Red Army as well as south through Italy and west through France by the Western Allies. Sweden was a handy sphere within which there could be mutual communication between diplomats from each side.

The camp at Theresienstadt was continually being used as a propaganda showcase to the wider world to convince everyone that the Jews were resettled in a relatively comfortable situation. To achieve this impression, they introduced various shops in late 1942 and even a café in December 1943. However, when the Danish King, Gustav X, demanded that there should be a visit in December 1943, the Nazis began a programme of 'beautification' involving sprucing up and painting all the barracks and other buildings even changing the name of the camp to Jewish Settlement Theresienstadt!

Before the visit the SS staff cleared out over 7,000 inmates straight to the death camps ensuring that the facilities looked their best and that only a few inmates were sharing the rooms. It was obviously a gigantic confidence trick to fool the inspectors who swallowed it hook, line and sinker. They clearly expected to see the equivalent terrible conditions currently being experienced in Warsaw. Following the visit, the SS even made a propaganda film entitled 'The Leader gives the Jews a town as a Gift' to show how well the Jews were being treated in what they presented as a 'Spa Town' where elderly Jews retired and engaged in cultural and musical pursuits. The brutal reality was that those involved in making and starring in the film were despatched to the Auschwitz-Birkenhau gas chambers as soon as it was completed.

Lizzy remembers this episode very clearly. When the Swiss inspectors came, the inmates suddenly got better food and she once got a ticket to the cabaret. She enjoyed this brief escapist interlude but could not remember the name of the show. After the inspectors left, life went back to what it was before which was like hell on earth.

Now the Nazis decided that all men under 55 years of age were to be transferred to another camp. This meant Lizzy's father Moric was deported on 8 September 1944 ostensibly to build a new camp elsewhere. He was only just within the age range by two months. Such were the mercurial fortunes of that war.

As all the men were gathered together to be put into the trucks to take them no family members were allowed to see them go.

However, Lizzy somehow managed to squeeze unnoticed through a door and to sneak into the crowded square, finding her father. They were able to spend a few precious moments together saying their goodbyes. She never saw him again or heard news of him. After the war she found out he had died in the Auschwitz-Birkenau killing chambers on 28 September 1944, only twenty days later. So much for the lie that they were to be taken to help build a new camp.

Auschwitz

Now it was Lizzy's turn. On 1 October 1944, she was sent away from Theresienstadt and joined a large number of Jews who were being transported over several days in those dreadful cattle trucks to Auschwitz. As ever they were crushed into an enclosed space without daylight, so much so, that her glasses got broken and she could hardly see in front of her face. She was devastated and felt totally helpless without being able to see. At the next camp they gave her a large load of glasses and got her to choose a pair. They were far from ideal but at least she could see what was going on around her. On arrival at Auschwitz, they were faced with large dogs, were lined up and all their possessions taken from them. All their hair was shaved off.

We now know that this and other human remains were used by the Germans to make various products for the people back in Germany. Now herded into bare barracks they had to sleep on bunk beds of wooden boards, ten to a bed with only one thin blanket between them all.

Auschwitz was the notorious death camp complex in southern Poland close to a railway which was constructed to fulfil the Nazi extermination policy. This was the camp where the camp doctor Joseph Mengele performed cruel experiments on the inmates, involving exposure to toxic substances, electroshocks and hypothermia especially focussing on twins. He was never brought to justice.

At his post-war Nuremburg trial, the camp commandant from 1940-43 estimated that 2.5 million persons had been killed there and another half a million had died from disease. He later reduced this figure as he had been unable to record all but the largest operations. He was hanged in Poland in April 1947.

Although difficult to identify exact numbers of those killed here owing to the burning of corpses and destruction of records as the Soviets approached, it is generally agreed that there were between 900,000 and 1.1 million Jewish victims, the figure published by the Auschwitz-Birkenau State Museum.

Somehow, Lizzy again managed to survive all the privations and the desperate selection queues which literally meant survival or death by an immediate choice by the guards. Life in these horrific camps was nothing short of the result of a constant series of sheer chances but Lizzy thinks that being young and with a bit more stamina helped her to survive these ordeals. Yet another lucky break.

Whilst at Auschwitz, the daily routine was getting up at 4am when they were literally chased out by the guards shouting: 'Raus! Raus!' (Out! Out!). Then they had to stand in lines to be counted. This often took up to five hours in the bitter cold with many of the already hungry and emaciated collapsing and some dying, thus aiding the Nazis' overall objective, extermination.

Auschwitz Entrance

They were allowed only two latrine breaks a day and sometimes the female guards forgot, often deliberately. Lizzy said to me that if they wanted to go to the toilet station outside these visits then it was just too bad. So many had to go on the earth floor of the barracks, clearly a nasty outcome. Throughout all this time as she was getting older, she was increasingly living in constant fear of the gas chambers which were very close to the barracks. Regularly the inmates would observe whole transports of people being taken to them. They knew their fate.

However, in the face of this daily terror, Lizzy later said she somehow always believed deep down that this terrible nightmare would end one day and she would finally go home. Despite the rumours and the contradictory evidence of her own eyes she also hoped against hope that she would be reunited with her family at the end of it all. This is indeed a remarkably inspiring statement of hope in the midst of what was a totally degrading inhuman situation without any possibility of escape. All the inmates were confined to the barracks and the bunks and anyone leaving the confines was shot on sight. Now, she developed a very painful furunculosis, a condition producing boils.

One day several SS men appeared in the barracks and they were ordered to undress and parade naked in front of them. They were separating the women into two groups, one to the left and one to the right. They were all very frightened that this was it: they were going to the gas chamber. She cannot actually remember the significance of which side was allocated to the gas chamber but she said she was obviously in the lucky one as she lived to tell her story.

A few days later Lizzy learned that her group was being sent away from Auschwitz. Once again, squashed together in the dreaded enclosed cattle trains they travelled through the unseen countryside and finally arrived in Dresden. There, they were required to work in a factory making parts for planes. The accommodation was marginally better, doubtless to help them work harder but the routine was typically soulless. They went from the barracks to the factory and then back again: nothing else. They were still hungry.

With their army now clearly losing the war and in full retreat in Poland, the German population began to panic about the advancing Red Army. They dreaded the inevitable revenge that would certainly be visited upon them. After what the *Einsatzgruppen* (Paramilitary Death Squads operating under the SS) had done in the Ukraine and other parts of Soviet Union, all Germans in the east were now getting very jumpy. The SS particularly had reason to be fearful as to their fate when the Allies entered the occupied territories. They desperately started to hide the evidence of their inhuman crimes in the extermination camps and elsewhere by all means possible. They dug up mass graves and burned corpses spreading the ashes around in the forests. In Terezin, the ashes of about 22,000 victims of the Holocaust were thrown into the River Ohře.

While Lizzy and her fellow inmates were working in Dresden, the Royal Air Force carpet bombed the city over three nights in February 1945 and their group had to hide. Lizzy recalls that they could see the sky lit up in flames, calling it the red sky. Because of the constant bombing, they were evacuated from the factory, partly walking and partly in transport. The walk was very tough with people collapsing all around from hunger and exhaustion. Strangely, she still never doubted it would end. Now, with the US Army also closing in, it was decided to move them even further away from Dresden. Partly walking and again in the infamous cattle trains they reached Mauthausen Camp, near Linz in Austria, about 20 kilometres to the south of the Czechoslovak border. Now more than ever the Jews lived in greater fear of being put to death by the soon to be defeated Nazis who were lashing out in all directions.

....

GATEWAY TO SPAIN

One November morning a relaxed and fully recuperated Jerzy was looking out of the hotel window where they were billeted to check on the weather. He recoiled stunned. As he says in his own words: "*I had the shock of my life!*" There were heavily armed German troops everywhere in the streets below. What was happening? The Germans had walked into the unoccupied zone. It was now occupied like the rest of France. They did not know why. They were now as tense this day as they had been relaxed the day before. "*We had to get out of there at once!*"

The larger background to his big shock was that on 11 November 1942 the Germans crossed the line between the zones and occupied the whole of France and Corsica, previously under the puppet jurisdiction of the Vichy Régime. This was a direct response to the Anglo-American invasion of French North Africa a few days before on 8 November, in conjunction with the westward thrust of the British Eighth Army, the Desert Rats, under General Montgomery.

While the Polish comrades were urgently getting ready to move on again, across the border to Andorra and then Spain, a bigger drama was being played out internationally. The French Fleet at Toulon, under Vichy control, had remained inactive during the Armistice period but now Hitler wanted to use it for control of the Mediterranean in response to the recent Anglo-American threat in North Africa.

However, the naval top brass decided now the time had come to support the real Free French forces under General De Gaulle so the fleet was scuttled and blown up with the loss of seventy seven vessels, whilst the submarines escaped to the coast of recently liberated North Africa. The furious Germans arrived too late. This was the end of collaborationist control in France. However, as far as the Polish comrades were concerned, they might as well be back in Germany itself. The previously safe zone was now fully occupied by the Germans and now dangerous yet again for the escapees.

It was now imperative to get these escapees away from there urgently. The group, now up to 32 in number, were quickly given directions to the Spanish border, issued with currency, change of underwear, outer clothes and strong walking boots. They would need the latter to help negotiate the rocky paths and uneven ridges.

"The French were very fantastic. I cannot criticise Pétain because he was doing what he could. They were doing everything they could to help us," Jerzy said after the war but also commented in passing that Pierre Laval, then Vichy Prime Minister: *"was a bastard."* It was not surprising he thought this as Laval had willingly sent Jews under the age of sixteen to the Nazis, even though they were exempted from transportation.

A controversial figure, Laval's overzealous anti-Semitism even shocked the local German authorities and the SS, certainly not known for their racial tolerance. He also enthusiastically aided and abetted the compulsory transfer of over 300,000 French workers to the occupied zone during his term of office.

While the world looked to the drama in Toulon, the recently adopted demobbed French-Polish companions were already surreptitiously making their way to Spain. They had to hike over the unwelcome terrain of the snow-capped Pyrenees mountain range during daylight on one of the 'Freedom Trails' with their supplies in small rucksacks. Being as they were going across in late autumn the snow was very thick on the ground which made each step sink in it adding to the overall effort.

It had to be done in daylight because walking across this treacherous ground at night was almost impossible for fear of stumbling and falling into a ravine or worse. In daylight, this journey was also fraught with the constant danger of discovery by the many German air patrols or Vichy French Milice (militia) land patrols or prior betrayal by some collaborator. In either case, the first the escapees would know about it would be the sudden appearance of the authorities in large numbers. Despite this potential threat and the fact that they were a sizeable group, they just had to keep going for as long as possible before nightfall. Fortunately, as army POWs, they were quite fit for this challenging task which was not the case for the many civilians who also attempted this trek in ordinary shoes. All the groups attempting these hazardous routes had to have a guide and there were many locals willing to help those fleeing the Nazis. Our Polish contingent travelled for 48 hours over the mountain pass.

On the way they drank the pure clear spring water which invigorated them and kept them positive in their task. At night they lit a small fire and sat round it, keeping warm: "*The night in the Pyrenees was something to remember ... the feeling of freedom, that's what complete freedom is I suppose, complete freedom is euphoric, incredibly exciting, in the mountains ...we lit a bonfire on top of the mountain, with clear, very tasty water, we were drinking this water like something very special. The guide was one of us ... Adam Gagolinski ... I know him and I'm in touch with him always.*" Sitting on the crest of the Pyrenees they felt they were sitting on top of the world as they contemplated their future free passage to Britain.

In the morning of the third day, they came down off the mountain into Andorra. The 32-strong group arrived at the Andorran border like "*almost like an invasion*" said Jerzy. Amazingly, before this they had seen no police or officials in the mountains but now there were eight policemen facing them. Clearly outnumbered, the Andorrans wanted no confrontation. Just then suddenly someone appeared who spoke Polish. He played host to them and took the group to a nearby hotel where they were treated to hot baths and food and a bed for the night. It transpired that this man had special funds to arrange this hospitality, so he was clearly au fait with some sort of advance-warning group.

Once again someone had appeared who spoke Polish. In Jerzy's mind he thought it strange that there seemed to be Polish speaking people appearing on their route at crucial moments. Was this coincidental or deliberate? Not only that but there were many French people and others as well forming a huge clandestine communication system dedicated to helping all opponents of the Nazis. Whilst this did not explain their lucky escapes from those close shaves at Moulins and Liège, once contact *had* been made, they were clearly under the wing of La Résistance, many of whom coincidentally could talk to them in their own language. It later transpired that there were a great many Poles in France who were part of a large covert underground organisation who were aiding escapees.

The next day the weather continued to be good for their planned crossing of the Andorran border into neutral Spain. Although technically a neutral country, wartime Spain was sympathetic to Nazi Germany. General Francisco Franco was the dictator whose Falangists had seized control of the country in a right-wing coup d'état in 1939 after three years of civil war with the legitimate Republican government. During the Spanish Civil War, he had received much support from the Nazis particularly in the bombing of the Basque town of Guernica by the Condor Legion of the Luftwaffe in April 1937, an outrage that shocked Europe and the world. This was subsequently the subject of a movingly stark painting by Pablo Picasso in June of that year which received a worldwide audience and focussed attention on the situation in Spain and the rise of Fascism. Franco is generally believed to have had over

200,000 political opponents killed in those years. They are still stumbling on many graves of those opponents of his army.

However, because of its status of official neutrality, Spain became a hot bed of intrigue and spying by all sides of Europe's political spectrum. More importantly for the comrades it also acted as the southern escape route for those who could make it across the rugged tough mountainous boundary. There were very few roads in this region but rather they were little more than rough paths through the rugged terrain. What a sight they must have been, this group of over thirty plus stumbling down these Pyrenean slopes meeting and greeting a few shepherds on the way in the bright early morning sunshine. As the descent continued, they turned around a bend in the very narrow path and saw Spanish soldiers armed with machine guns waiting for them. They clearly knew that they were coming down from the mountain. A tense moment occurred but despite initial appearances the soldiers turned out to be friendly and asked the Poles to join them. In the group were a couple of Jewish Cadets and Jerzy said that: *"They had already been fished out by the Spaniards,"* who were standing and looking for who next was coming around the corner.

When the next two comrades came down the narrow path dancing with their hands up to surrender, everyone burst out laughing. All tension immediately vanished.

The atmosphere was positively friendly and our recently 'demobilised' Frenchmen were put onto large trucks with guards and taken to the nearest town where they were received and welcomed by the Mayor and treated to a full-scale banquet with wine and a wide choice of food, music and with some Spanish girls who were dancing. "*We ate to oblivion*" Jerzy said after their tough walk and meagre survival rations. They all agreed it was a reception beyond all expectations.

The group had successfully negotiated that Freedom Trail, which was an impressive feat, given the terrain. The route was through the Ariège section of the Pyrenees, a tough uneven path across the mountains, reaching heights of over 2,500 metres, relatively safe from Nazi-Vichy surveillance although now increasing after their occupation of the southern zone. These particular escape routes were used by over thirty thousand French people and Jews fleeing the Nazis between 1940 and 1944, as well as six thousand allied servicemen and pilots who been shot down.

The following day a new set of not so friendly Spanish troops came to meet them and took them down to the lower parts of the countryside in trucks carrying timber. They sat on top of the logs and each truck had a Spanish guard accompanying it. In the town the euphoric atmosphere of the previous day suddenly changed.

They were shut inside a prison in the Catalonian town of Llieda, out of the French 'frying pan into the Spanish fire'. Without any recognised warning they had crossed an international border and so were clearly regarded as suspicious aliens. In the meantime, Jerzy learned he must not declare himself as a Pole but as a Canadian of Polish origin. With the help of some local clerks they quickly learned to adapt to the new requirements. Over seven days they were kept in Llieda. In 1996, Jerzy commented: *"I think my fingerprints are there still."* After the end of that week the British Consul visited them bringing food supplies which they desperately needed.

Later, Jerzy says, they: *"Were transported to the Concentratione at Miranda de Ebro where all the foreigners were but then I was under the protection of the British."* This somewhat scruffy handwritten note is written confirmation in French that the leader of a Canadian group certifies that Jerzy (referred to as George) stopped off as part of that group between 26 November 1942 and 17 April 1943.

Canadian Group membership

They were eventually released and taken to the British Embassy in Madrid. Lord Hoare, who Jerzy thought was in charge there, (in fact the British Ambassador) came to welcome them. Then they were put on a train and travelled right across Spain south to La Linea just across from Gibraltar. Jerzy was led across to Gibraltar by Major Count Lubienski, Head of the Polish Naval Mission and father of the future actress Rula Lenska.

The Spanish Trek

● ● ● ● ● ● ● ●

LIZZY'S LIBERATION

Finally, after all her fear and suffering, on 5 May 1945, the Americans arrived at the camp gates of Mauthausen main concentration camp. It was liberated by a platoon of 23 men from the 11th Armoured Division of the US Third Army, led by Staff Sergeant. Albert J. Kosiek. There was a supreme feeling of relief and joy and they shook hands and crowded around the soldiers. There was however a problem because the soldiers had to be careful about feeding them rich food as there were some serious problems of digestion caused by many years of near starvation, so it was only soup to begin with. This particularly applied to the very ill and malnourished inmates mainly the old and infirm. The SS guards had already fled, afraid of reprisals from the inmates.

The horrendous ordeal was finally over. Lizzy has said she always believed that, somehow, she would survive this hell on earth. Now she had. Her hope was realised. She had spent four years between the ages of 14 and 18 in those foul Nazi concentration camps. It was an unimaginably terrible time for a teenager who had gone from a carefree existence before the war for it to be replaced by casual cruelty, endless hunger and a constant fear for the future day by day, minute by minute. Her teenage years, when most would be developing in so many necessary ways were severely blighted by this and even now in mature years later, she cannot forget what happened to her family just because she happened to be Jewish.

Asked how she feels about Germans today she says she still feels an antipathy to them, particularly the older generation. Naturally, she is still haunted by the fate of her parents and sister. All her family perished by violence and inhumane treatment: her mother Hilda Schwarz, née Spielmann, from malnourishment and inadequate healthcare in Theresienstadt, on 14 June 1942, her sister Kitty in the Auschwitz gas chambers on 6 September 1943 and her father Moric Schwarz in the Auschwitz gas chambers on 28 September 1944.

Coming to terms with that horrific experience is nigh impossible yet Lizzy has since made a positive life for herself since that time, meeting and marrying her escapee husband and having two daughters.

Unsurprisingly, she has forgotten many specific details of these horrific and grotesque events that are a stain on the twentieth century, having clearly consigned these unspeakable experiences into the deepest recesses of her mind. However, despite this fully understandable mental block and the apparent matter-of-fact descriptions of those dreadful times, it must be clear to any modern listener or reader that these circumstances have been seared forever into her memory. It is to her credit that she has been able to move on and enjoy her life far away from the abhorrent dictatorship that was Hitler and his Nazi thugs.

Today she says that it is terrible to realise that it was not a nightmare but that it all actually happened.

Lizzy, Kitty and Hilda Schwarz

. . . .

UNIFORM AGAIN

The 'Canadian' comrades landed in Gibraltar in December 1942 and became Polish Officer Cadets again as they were supplied with new military uniforms by the Polish Mission there. Over three months, the escapees had travelled over 2,200 miles all the way across Belgium, France and Spain on both foot and public transport. On the way they had lucky breaks and help from those at risk of death but had now arrived safely in British territory. Jerzy was in Gibraltar for six months and in June 1943 was flown to Greenock in Scotland. After the excitement and sunshine of Spain and Gibraltar he was somewhat unimpressed saying:" *It was a bit of a comedown.*" Obviously, by then he had learned the subtle art of the British understatement!

Then he was taken down to the south of England where they were screened, the regular debriefing of military personnel who had been through enemy territory, in order to cull any useful information: what they had seen, troop movements, air raids and so on. This was at the Patriotic School at Latchmere House, near Richmond Park, where he lived while taking English lessons: "*Taught by British people speaking excellent Polish*". Thereafter, he was inducted into the Royal

Signals Corps and sent back to Scotland to be trained in electronic communications at Auchtermuchty.

Eventually, with improving English, a few propositions were put to him by the authorities. He could choose to go back to Poland, join the Special Operations Executive (SOE), a secret unit engaged in espionage, sabotage and reconnaissance behind enemy lines, or join the forces in Scotland.

"*I wanted to join the RAF but it didn't work out for health reasons.*" For the time being he stayed in Scotland in the Royal Signals Corps and trained in electronic communications. Gradually the group of those original escapees was disbanded as they were sent to various postings in other places.

Later, it was suggested to him that he join the unit which was to organise airfields behind enemy lines in northern France before the D-Day invasion in June 1944 and he was sent on a technology course at Northampton Polytechnic at that time. From his 1990's interview it is unclear whether Jerzy took up this offer and there is no available documentation as to whether he did go behind enemy lines.

During 1944 and 1945 Jerzy was in London. "*I was stationed in London all the time. The first place was a hotel somewhere in Bayswater ... at the time there were flying bombs. When the V2 fell on Tottenham Court Road I was in Oxford Street at that time. I didn't realise what it was actually ... nothing showed what had happened.*" He learned it fell on Tottenham Court Road later.

What he described here is the final vengeful throw of the Nazi dice. Just when the British began to relax, thinking the war to be nearly over, the Germans launched the V1 flying bombs from a base in the Pas-de-Calais in June 1944 just after the D-Day invasion in Normandy. Visions of the terrible Blitz of 1940 returned to everyone's consternation. Known colloquially as 'doodlebugs' because of the strange intermittent droning sound they made, which resembled a two-stroke motor bike engine, they were basically early jet-propelled cruise missiles. Nearing the target, they fell silent some seconds before dropping to earth, at which point everyone in the vicinity dived for cover hoping they would escape the inevitable explosion. A seemingly endless stream of these weapons struck terror into the local population of London and the South East, killing just over 6,000 people. As if this was not enough, they were closely followed by the V2 rockets in September even more devastating in power and terrifying effect because they were silent until impact. Walking along Oxford Street Jerzy had obviously experienced the huge explosion of one of these V2s.

He did not have a clue what it was. One moment life was going on, the next, absolute oblivion for those beneath, sudden silent death from the skies. The V2s killed over 7,500 people.

The Nazis described these as 'revenge weapons' and they were a desperate attempt to get the Western Allies to sue for peace and to save the Nazis from the rapidly advancing Red Army and their recriminations on the Eastern Front. Devastating though the rockets were, they failed in the end to achieve their aim, owing to the sharp shooting of the RAF pilots and subterfuge by the government and the media, which leaked false information based on phoney coordinates about the success of the attacks. The Germans fell for the ruse, directing future launches on 'targets' in the deserted countryside around the capital, thus saving many lives.

At the end of the war demobilisation occurred and some of the original members of the unit went on to continue their previously intended electronic studies in universities.

Jerzy back in uniform, London, 1945

. . . .

POLISH RESETTLEMENT CORPS

In 1945, with the Red Army pushing the Germans out of Poland on their westward advance to Berlin, the future of the country was in the balance. At the immediate post-war Potsdam Conference, Britain and the United States acceded to Soviet leader Stalin's forcible demands that the Soviet Union be rewarded for their war efforts by gaining vast tracts of Eastern Europe. This particularly applied to previously divided Poland under the secret Nazi-Soviet Pact of 1939 before they were at war. At the conference it was agreed by UK Prime Minister Winston Churchill and US President Franklin Roosevelt that there would be a Provisional Government in Poland until democratic elections could be held. Of course Stalin, a ruthless dictator like his adversary Hitler, reneged on the agreement and set up a contrived government full of communists, thus producing the conditions for Poland to become a communist satellite state for over forty years. The proper Polish Government in exile never forgave the British or Americans for this 'western betrayal', especially as Britain had gone to war to save Poland from the Nazi invasion in the first place.

A year later, the British Government formed the Polish Resettlement Corps to help the 180,000 Polish personnel serving with the British forces who did not wish to return to a communist dominated Poland. It was run by the British Army and served to ease them into civilian life until they were fully adjusted to it.

Obviously, as a serving officer, Jerzy was included in this organisation. He was one of 2,000 located at the Witley Camp near Godalming, Surrey. The PRC was eventually disbanded in 1949 and Jerzy received confirmation of the relinquishing of his commission in a letter dated 12 July that year.

In entry to post-war civilian life, Jerzy became a structural engineer which had been his original intention after his compulsory military service in Poland. He decided to remain in London. "*I stayed in London because I was warned by my father not to come* (back to Poland). *It was always my aim to get to England because of the culture, the way of life.*"

Directly after the war, aside from Poland, the Soviet-backed Communists gained ultimate power in the other eastern countries of Europe by similar dubious means, manipulating and fixing the elections in East Germany, Czechoslovakia, Hungary, Bulgaria and Romania. Yugoslavia was the exception developing its own semi-independent form of communism and refusing to bow to Soviet control. It is little wonder that, in these circumstances, Jerzy did not want to return to his homeland.

....

MEETING LIZZY

Living now in Fulham, Jerzy was introduced to Lizzy who was a friend of a Polish couple who lived in the same house as him. At that time he had no idea about her wartime experiences.

Shortly after they met, her only remaining relative Aunt Lily who had fled Czechoslovakia in 1939, was killed in a fire in a London music publishing business in Gerrard Street.

Jerzy accompanied Lizzy to the mortuary so she could identify her aunt and after that they became close friends. He began to take an interest in her and after many years of courting they eventually got married on 17 September 1955. He still did not know her devastating family history which had been as dreadfully inhuman as his was dangerously dramatic. She did not talk about it for a long time.

Later in their relationship, Lizzy very gradually spoke about her parents and her wartime history of lucky escapes from the concentration camps: *She did not want to talk about these things for a long time but later when she talked about her parents it came out they were in the Holocaust.*

They went to Czechoslovakia a few times and revisited Poland once in later years for a holiday but Jerzy has said he did not feel he belonged there anymore and felt like a stranger in what had been his homeland. He also recounts he had a friend who: *"sounds like a Polish Scotsman!"* clearly the result of their stay in Scotland after their escape.

Talking about his experiences as a POW and the escapes, he regretted that: *"I haven't been back to those places involved in my escape but the thing which I regret is I couldn't make contact with that brave Polish family in Liège who were so brilliant."* They were the ones who put them up right next door to the Gestapo Head-quarters. That episode in Liège epitomised the continuous run of pulse-raising lucky coincidences which summed up Cadet Officer, now Second Lieutenant Jerzy Henryk Dyszkiewicz's short military career and alternative occupation as an escape artist, on his way to becoming George Henry Dyszkiewicz, British Citizen. Although they had been captured, swapped between different forces, he and his comrades refused to give up and accept the status of prisoners of war. They planned thoroughly and exhibited great courage by achieving a daring escape followed by a thrilling yet dangerous trail to ultimate freedom.

The photo below, shows how integrated and dashing in demeanour George became in post-war civilian life with his English trench coat and pipe.

POST-WAR LIFE

Soon after her liberation from the camp Lizzy travelled in trucks to Prague and from there went home by train to her birth town: Boskovice. When she arrived at her original home, she found, to her surprise, that her nanny was still living in the house. The nanny had stayed there and served the Germans, at the same time keeping a watch over the house. When she walked from the station to her home, she could not believe it was happening and was happy to be finally free from the oppressive threatening precarious existence of the last four years.

Hope is a wonderful feeling, one of expectation. On this day she was filled with hope against hope that her father would be there having been liberated like her. She knew her sister Kitty was almost certainly dead because that was the fate of inmates transported to Auschwitz, known to be one of the worst death camps. However, she did not specifically know her father's fate although she suspected it. Later it was confirmed that he too had died in the camps.

Although relieved at her own survival she was overwhelmed by a deep sadness in realising that she now had no close family left. It is impossible to imagine that final relief heavily tinged with desolation and loneliness. She was just eighteen years old and had incredibly survived a maelstrom of degrading and inhumane experiences at the hands of the most heinous Nazi criminals. She was now completely alone in the post-war world of Czechoslovakia. Her sister had been gassed at twenty years old and there were only five Jews left in her town from all the thousands that had been deported and exterminated in the death camps.

With great difficulty, she settled back into a relatively normal existence and followed a two-year secretarial course learning shorthand typing and accounts in a commercial college. While in Boskovice she and her nanny contacted her father's sister, aunt Lilly, her only living immediate family relative who lived in England. In response, she was invited to go to live with Lilly in London. Lilly had been one of the many Jews who had read the ominous signs about the Munich crisis and migrated from Czechoslovakia.

At first Lizzy was reluctant about this because she was in a state of confusion not knowing what best to do about her future. She was happy that the war and her own terrible experiences were over but very sad about those years spent struggling in the dreadful camps. Eventually, in 1947, she went to England to see her aunt Lilly and flew to Blackbushe Aerodrome in Hampshire. She disembarked with a note around her neck, saying 'not speaking English'. Her aunt was not there to meet her! Lizzy was panicking.

Once again though, her lucky coincidences kicked in. A very nice English gentleman who had worked in Prague a year or two before the war and who spoke some Czech gave her some money and phoned her aunt. She had sent Lilly a telegram saying which flight she was on but had forgotten to say which airport she was arriving at! All ended well though. She took a coach to Kensington to meet Lilly.

Once resident in Fulham with her aunt, Lizzy signed on at Pitman's College and found work as a secretary. She had her Home office visa extended again and again until she was eventually granted residency and made England her permanent home. All in her life now seemed to be improving after her wartime ordeal but more bad news was just around the corner.

One Friday evening, in November 1950, the police called at the house to say her aunt had perished in a fire at her workplace. She worked in an old building in the City and had gone upstairs to wash her hands before leaving work when a fire broke out. It consumed the old wooden staircase and she could not get down quick enough before it took hold. Having left Czechoslovakia just before the Nazis invaded and occupied the country in 1939, with disastrous consequences for the rest of her family, it is terribly sad that Lilly should then die eleven years later in what was an avoidable accident in her newly adopted home. Now Lizzy was completely alone in London without any family left.

Aunt Lilly

This was yet another blow for Lizzy, to lose her only relative after all she had been through. Now though there was a positive twist of fate. While sharing a house in Swiss Cottage with two other holocaust survivors, Edith and Helen, Lizzy met and became friendly with a Polish man, Jerzy. In her grief, this Polish man looked after her and went to the mortuary with her to identify her aunt. He was Jerzy, the very same Polish Officer Cadet whose daring escape exploits have been described earlier. After this adventure full of lucky coincidences, he too had eventually arrived and settled in London. Although he did not know that at the time, Lizzy was a Holocaust survivor.

Lizzy had suffered horrific inhuman experiences with the endless life-threatening pressure of an unknown fate: would she live to survive another day? Would she be selected for the gas chamber by a throw of the selection dice? Given that tenuous existence, it is hardly surprising that Lizzy began to embrace her post-war freedom to the full. Her newly found carefree attitude which coincidentally relives her childhood is aptly captured in the photo below on Brighton Beach. It is the smile and demeanour of the incredibly lucky survivor with everything to live for.

After the war Lizzy ironically worked for a Czech lawyer handling claims against Germany mainly for loss of property which involved translating documents and letters between clients and Germany for compensation claims. All the clients got their money. She said she had no feelings about it because it was just a job that had to be done.

Eventually, Lizzy, the lucky Jewish survivor of the camps, married Jerzy, the Roman Catholic Polish POW and escapee in 1955 and they initially lived in a flat in Chiswick. She worked from 1949 until her first daughter Caroline was born in June 1962. Another daughter Nicola was born in June 1965.

Lizzy and George's Wedding

· · · · · · · ·

POSTSCRIPT

The chance meeting between Lizzy and George in post-war London was the culmination of a series of previous lucky events on both their journeys. Their wedding was a double miracle. Lizzy survived the camps against all odds. Jerzy now George had been extricated from many close shaves while on the run. Both could have been killed at any time: Lizzy in the selection queues or from disease or starvation and George if captured in civilian clothes being tortured then executed as an enemy spy.

They moved to a small cul-de-sac in a South West London suburb and raised a family. Their neighbours are all close friends and they have regular get-togethers on various occasions. Lizzy has retained her Jewish identity in a secular rather than religious sense. She has done charity work by volunteering in an old people's home and running a shop every Wednesday.

Lizzy returned to Prague and Boskovice in 1988. She received a wonderful reception and the locals remembered her family. Given her experiences in pre-war days her old school friends could not have been nicer to her. She returned there again in 1990 with her two daughters.

On a trip to Theresienstadt Cemetery there were hundreds of memorial stones all in the same design but no sign of her family grave. It was a very sad place and her grown-up daughters felt that the atmosphere was eerie. This is a common reaction in these cemeteries and camps where visitors report a strange stillness in the air, a lack of birdsong and normal plant growth.

She later pushed for a family stone to be erected. The inscription succinctly states that her family perished during the war. All negotiations were conducted by post but she has not seen it first-hand.

The nanny who guarded the family home during the occupation eventually advised Lizzy to sell it. Sadly, the debts accrued over years cancelled out any profit from the sale. There were some funds in a Prague bank for over 25 years but they would not send it or pay any interest as it was a foreign account. Lizzy had to go there to collect it and it paid for the trip in 1988.

Apart from her daughters, Lizzy has an extended family of some cousins. These are her mother's brother's children who came to England on the Kindertransport. One now lives in Connecticut, one in Newbury, Berkshire and one in Dubai. They keep in regular touch and as they all have children there are plenty of family communications and meetings.

CONCLUSION

Our two protagonists could not have come from more different backgrounds. Lizzy was a Czechoslovakian Jew and Jerzy a Roman Catholic Pole. They are linked in history by the events of 1939.

In the March, Lizzy and her family were coming to terms with the German occupation of their country and the threats they faced being Jewish, resulting from Nazi racial policy.

In the September, recently qualified Officer Cadet Jerzy was confidently marching with his unit to meet the German invader. To their surprise they were surrounded and captured by the Red Army Cavalry coming in from the East and were shipped off to the Ukraine, eventually to be handed over to the Germans.

Life for Lizzy and her family rapidly deteriorated into an intolerable downward spiral. Severe limits were increasingly imposed on their lives until they were eventually rounded up and transported to a concentration camp and eventually onto Auschwitz, where the rest of her family perished. Thereafter, Lizzy's life was a terrifying journey through the camps never knowing what would happen to her, day to day, minute by minute, living in constant fear subject to the whims of the guards. She thinks she survived because of her youth and usefulness as a worker.

Jerzy and three close army comrades were transported around Germany as illegal labourers doing menial manual jobs, without pay, in contradiction of the Geneva Convention. In one camp, close to the Belgian border, they executed their escape plan and travelled undercover, a roller coaster of apprehension facing many dangerous situations throughout France and onto neutral Spain and Gibraltar.

Appendix A shows their relative events and Appendix B their journeys enforced upon them by the external circumstances of war-torn Europe. Coincidentally, Appendix B shows they both passed through Brno and Vienna but at different times. Jerzy's line is the busier because the Germans were continually moving their POWs around to many places to suit the demands for casual slave labour. In contrast, Lizzy's line has very few recorded points of contact as she was confined in fewer places, completely at the mercy of decisions taken by the camp authorities.

The facts about the mass killing of Jews and others in Poland and the USSR first emerged in late 1941 and was further elaborated throughout 1942, as word got out to London. It is estimated that over 700,000 Jews had already been murdered in the Chelmno extermination camp in Poland long before the mass killings later that occurred as the Nazis moved East. Some historical critics think the allies initially turned a blind eye to what they believed was unthinkable behaviour by a civilised European society.

In the passage of too much time though, any lingering doubt was dispelled as the full horror of this industrialised scale of murder became crystal clear as the allies closed in on Germany from both West and East and encountered the horror of the death camps.

The truth of this today is that this revolting scar on the history of humanity is now forever burnt into our contemporary consciousness. Sadly, there are those, who for some perverted reason choose to deny its very existence, despite clear evidence.

In summarising these events, it is very important here to challenge the idea that ordinary Germans did not really have any firm knowledge that this policy was being enacted. This has been variously refuted in recent years, particularly so by Robert Galletely, in *Backing Hitler: Consent and Coercion in Nazi Germany*. Based upon a thorough study of the news media at the time, he makes a very clear argument showing that the German people were either generally indifferent or openly approved of Nazis' Darwinist racial policies. Because of this the Nazis were able to implement their disgusting treatment of at least six million Jews, of which a million were innocent children. This is not to mention millions of ethnic Poles, Soviet POWs and civilians, the Roma, disabled and gays, who followed the earlier communists, socialists, liberals and anyone else adjudged to be inferior, to the death camps.

Simultaneously, Nazi Propaganda Minister Josef Goebbels worked tirelessly to manipulate, deceive and deny the truth to the outside world. One of their most successful deceptions was in Theresienstadt where the teenage Lizzy was interned.

Thinking about all this, Lizzy puts her survival down to a continuing run of sheer luck, a split-second decision by some guard or other. Jerzy's trip through Europe was opportunistic as the laundress in Liège who hid the comrades next to the Gestapo Headquarters proved and the heart stopping moment at Moulins at the Vichy border showed. Later it appeared that the underground and resistance also played a hidden hand at times but this does not detract from his courage. Many helpers surprisingly spoke some Polish. The reason for this was that there were a big number of ex-patriot Poles in undercover resistance activities in France dating back to a big influx after the defeat of Poland in 1939.

These two people, complete strangers in culture, religion and geography during the war, met in London, became companions, eventually married and settled in suburban England, a whole world away from Czechoslovakia and Poland. This couple's stories stand the test of time despite being brought to us from another age long gone. Her husband George said: "*Whatever we went through we are a happy family.*" (Sadly, before I had a chance to meet him and discuss his great adventure, George died in Kingston-upon-Thames, aged 96 on 23 July 2016.)

Looking back on those events, Lizzy says that insignificant things do not bother her anymore, unsurprising given her experience. She has survived to tell her story to add to all the other death camp survivors' experiences: an indictment of racism. However, she is adamant that this must never be allowed to happen again. Even now, she observes, there are those who deny it. I was privileged to meet and talk to Lizzy personally and found her to be full of life in her nineties, regularly taking the bus to go shopping.

What lessons can we draw from these experiences? We must *never forget* what happened to all those victims of the vicious Nazi attack upon ordinary humanity to avoid any recurrence. We must listen to every survivor.

The 1990's genocide in Yugoslavia in the name of unfounded racial beliefs demonstrates that these views still lurk below the surface even in modern Europe. More recently, the current right-wing nationalist and fascistic resurgence in Europe over multiculturism and migration demonstrate that there are echoes of the thirties, even now. We should look at the history of the earlier events and challenge any such trends full on before they have a chance to take hold. This quote from unverified sources nevertheless sums up the danger: "*All that is necessary for the triumph of evil is that good people do nothing.*"

Finally, there is always hope in despair. Lizzy proved it and her story ended happily. A young German Jewish girl in Holland also believed it, although unlike Lizzy she did not survive the horrific Nazi Holocaust dying from typhus in Bergen-Belsen in 1945. We leave the last word to her:

"I've found that there is always some beauty left -- in nature, sunshine, freedom, in yourself; these can all help you."

Anne Frank, *The Diary of a Young Girl*, Doubleday, New York, 1952

....

APPENDIX A: THE JOURNEYS

	Jerzy	Lizzy
1938	Joined Officer Cadet School in Lodz	Parents worrying as "Hitler getting nearer and nearer"
1939		
15 March		Germany occupied/split Czechoslovakia
		Lizzy's Aunt Lilly left for England
1 Sept	Germany invaded Poland and Stukas bombed barracks	Lizzy's family stayed
28 Sept	Jerzy's unit surrounded by Soviet Army Cavalry, on train to Kiev, then Kharkov	
Oct	Exchanged with Germans with people 'crossing Bug River' On train to Austrian 'collection centre' near Vienna	
Dec	In Oflag VII-A POW camp at Murnau, Bavaria	
1940		Father called into Gestapo HQ in Brno, safe return, no explanation
June	Sent to 'punishment camp' somewhere in northern Holland	Lizzy removed from local school

	Jerzy	Lizzy
1941		
July		Lizzy attended Jewish Gymnasium in Brno
1 Sept		Jews had to wear Yellow Star on clothes
Later date		Germans commandeered the family shop, forced into back streets
		Jews assembled in Boskovice centre for deportation
		Interned in hall of big hotel in Brno,
		Lizzy's mother heart condition worsened
1941-2	Sent to Oflag VI-G POW camp, Hoffnungsthal, East of Cologne	
	Witnessed devastating bombing of the city at night	
1942		
19 March		Schwarz family transported by cattle train to Terezin (Theresienstadt concentration camp)
14 June		Lizzy's mother died, father and daughters allowed to attend group funeral
	Sent to Oflag VI-H POW camp, Rothe Erde, Aachen	
2 Oct	02.00 hours: Jerzy and 3 others escaped for Belgian border	
	04.00 hours, Slept during the day on a high hill	

	Jerzy	Lizzy
3 Oct	Walked in direction of Belgian border using self-made compass	
	Saw French signpost, now in Belgium, stayed with local doctor, in the 'underground'	
	Arrived in Liège at 7pm, met woman speaking broken Polish	
4 Oct	Taken back to house next to Gestapo HQ! Hid in loft at weekend	
5 Oct	Tram to Lille accompanied by a guide	
	At dentist's house, hid in garden office all day	
	Train to Amiens, had to sleep in a field	
6 Oct	Train to Paris to meet ex-POW friend, city full of soldiers, hotel overnight	
7 Oct	Train tickets to Lyon but had to alight stop before Moulins (Vichy border)	
	Missed stop so arrived Moulins for papers check, escaped this	
	In town 'Lady of the night' approached them, hid in vegetable shop	

	Lizzy	

	Jerzy	
7 Oct	Crossed over Allier River into 'zone libre'	
	Night and meal to remember!	
8 Oct	Slept in hayloft overnight	
9 Oct	Train to Auch, adopted demobbed French Army identity	
11 Nov	Germans entered unoccupied zone	
12 Nov	Journeyed to Aulus-les-Bains Polish Centre, Ariège Region	
27 Nov	Group of 32 issued with money and sturdy kit for Pyrenees trek	
1 Dec	Into Andorra and put up in hotel	
2 Dec	Descended into Spain and met by troops, taken to Pobla de Segur	
	Given reception by the Mayor	
3 Dec	Taken to Llieda and interned but clerks designated them Canadian	
10 Dec	Group visited by British Consul	
11 Dec	Group temporarily interned at Miranda de Ebro 'concentratione'	

	Jerzy	Lizzy
14 Dec	Group taken by train to Madrid, met British Ambassador	
15 Dec	Train from Madrid to La Linea and then across to Gibraltar	
1943		
June	Flown to Greenock, Scotland	
	Sent to Latchmere House, Ham, Surrey for debrief	
	Inducted into Royal Signal Corps, Auchtermuchty	
6 Sept		Lizzy's sister Kitty sent to Auschwitz gas chambers
1944		
23 June		International/Danish Red Cross inspected Theresienstadt
8 Sept		Lizzy's father deported to build another camp
28 Sept		Lizzy's father died in Auschwitz gas chambers
1 Oct		Lizzy sent to Auschwitz in cattle trucks
Date?		Sent to Dresden to work in aircraft factory

	Jerzy	Lizzy
1945		
Feb		Witnessed RAF carpet bombing of Dresden
		Moved to Mauthausen camp by walking and train
March	Jerzy witnessed V2 rocket hit Tottenham Court Road	
5 May		Mauthausen liberated by US Army
Soon after	Jerzy demobbed and became structural engineer	Travelled to Prague in a truck then Boskovice by train
1946	Formation of Polish Resettlement Corps	
1947		Completed 2-year Secretarial Course
		Visited Aunt Lilly in England in Fulham
8 Sept	Jerzy issued with Alien ID for stay/employment etc	
Sept		Attended Pitman's College
1949		Worked for Czech lawyer until first daughter born
12 July	Jerzy relinquished commission, entered civilian life	Jerzy meets Lizzy
1950		
Nov		Aunt Lilly died in a fire at work, no living relatives
1955		Jerzy marries Lizzy

APPENDIX B

Jerzy journey: Broken line

Lizzy journey: Unbroken line

THE AUTHOR

Ted Bailey is an ex-college and university teacher with an interest in history and culture. He is a published author of several books including one about the First World War in *A Major Soldier*, Reveille Press.

He encountered the basic facts of Lizzy and Jerzy's wartime experiences by sheer coincidence. Based on recorded interviews conducted with both protagonists many years ago he has pieced together their relative stories and set them into the wider historical context. It is important that we remember these events as a lesson for the future.